When Dan and Tremper get together it's just the best. This is even better for your soul than chicken soup.

JOHN ORTBERG
Senior pastor of Menlo Park Presbyterian Church and author of
All the Places to Go . . . How Will You Know?

This book shows that emotions are neither an embarrassment nor an impediment to spirituality, but the very stuff God uses as He shapes His salvation in us.

EUGENE H. PETERSON
Author of *The Message*

If we are to be rescued from the incessant tendency to psychologize the gospel, this book will be a good start. Dan and Tremper give us not more psychological information, but biblical encouragement to be faithful.

MICHAEL CARD
Singer, songwriter, and author of *Immanuel: Reflections on the Life of Christ*

Allender and Longman add an important contribution to a new wave of Psalm studies. There is an enormous temptation for "high faith" to deny the dark side of life where "things do not work." Against that common propensity, they show how the Psalms make contact with the emotions of failure. Such places in life become, by their sensitive reading of the Psalms, places of revelatory healing and transformation. Readers will be helped to fresh and faithful discernment of life and text.

WALTER BRUEGGEMANN
Professor of Old Testament, Columbia Theological Seminary

An excellent piece of scholarship suitable equally for the layperson and the theologian.

PUBLISHERS WEEKLY

Exactly what we need in a world of declining civility where pain, grief, and suffering seem to be increasing almost beyond our capacity to cope.

ANN APPLEGARTH
Virtue

The Cry of the Soul is a thoughtful book. It invites us to admit whatever we feel, to know that we're not alone in what we feel, but then to follow a path that our emotions illumine into a life-changing encounter with God. Its message is away from managing our feelings toward entering the mystery of our emotional life as a means of knowing the Lord more fully. And that's the message our world needs to hear.

LARRY CRABB
Christian counselor, author, and founder of New Way Ministries

Dan and Tremper have done us a fierce kindness. In a culture committed to either running from or wallowing in our emotions, *The Cry of the Soul* offers an excruciating but hopeful alternative— to listen to our own hearts (as did the psalmists) so we can better receive and worship the pursuing heart of God.

NANCY GROOM
Author of *From Bondage to Bonding*

The Cry of the Soul offers insight after surprising insight into the unexpected relationship between our emotions and our view of God. A needed correction to a simplistic explaining away of pain and suffering.

DANIEL TAYLOR
Author of *The Myth of Certainty*

In *The Cry of the Soul* I hear an echo of my own heart-cry and that of the psalmists—to know God intimately and authentically, and to see Him powerfully at work in our broken world.

LUCI SHAW
Author of *God in the Dark*

the cry of the soul

-

HOW OUR EMOTIONS REVEAL
OUR DEEPEST QUESTIONS ABOUT GOD

-

DR. DAN B. ALLENDER
DR. TREMPER LONGMAN III

-

A NavPress resource published in alliance
with Tyndale House Publishers, Inc.

NavPress is the publishing ministry of The Navigators, an international Christian organization and leader in personal spiritual development. NavPress is committed to helping people grow spiritually and enjoy lives of meaning and hope through personal and group resources that are biblically rooted, culturally relevant, and highly practical.

For more information, go to www.NavPress.com.

The Cry of the Soul: How Our Emotions Reveal Our Deepest Questions about God

Copyright © 1994 by Wounded Heart Ministries. All rights reserved.

Foreword copyright © 2015 by Joni Eareckson Tada. All rights reserved.

A NavPress resource published in alliance with Tyndale House Publishers, Inc.

NAVPRESS and the NAVPRESS logo are registered trademarks of NavPress, The Navigators, Colorado Springs, CO. *TYNDALE* is a registered trademark of Tyndale House Publishers, Inc., Carol Stream, IL. Absence of ® in connection with marks of NavPress or other parties does not indicate an absence of registration of those marks.

Designed by Faceout Studio, Jeff Miller

Cover photograph of chair copyright © Louis W/Shutterstock. All rights reserved.
Cover photograph of photo room copyright © coka/Shutterstock. All rights reserved.

Scripture taken from the Holy Bible, *New International Version,*® *NIV.*® Copyright © 1973, 1978, 1984, 2011 by Biblica, Inc.® (Some quotations may be from the earlier NIV edition, copyright © 1984.) Used by permission. All rights reserved worldwide.

Some of the anecdotal illustrations in this book are true to life and are included with the permission of the persons involved. All other illustrations are composites of real situations, and any resemblance to people living or dead is coincidental.

Library of Congress Cataloging-in-Publication Data

Allender, Dan B.
  The cry of the soul : how our emotions reveal our deepest questions about God / Dan B. Allender, Tremper Longman III.
    p. cm.
  Includes bibliographical references.
  ISBN 0-89109-827-5
  1. Emotions—Religious aspects—Christianity. 2. God. I. Longman, Tremper. II.-Title.
BV4597.3.A45 1994
248.2—dc20   94-14312
                                                                              CIP

ISBN 978-1-57683-180-9

Printed in the United States of America

21   20   19   18   17   16   15
 7   6   5   4   3   2   1

CONTENTS

In Memoriam
Dr. Raymond B. Dillard
1944–1993

FOREWORD:
BEFORE YOU BEGIN . . .

"I don't get it. I just don't understand God."

It was a comment I'd heard one other time from my coworker, Greg. Maybe the long drive to our workshop had gotten to him, with a still longer freeway ahead. I watched him from my wheelchair behind the driver's seat. Something told me he'd be more comfortable by a trout stream today than leading a disability workshop.

Greg is divorced and every once in a while the wound can seep. Like this afternoon. He has one hand on the wheel while stretching with the other to feed banana and crackers to his son. Ryan is his beautiful ten-year-old boy with the happy smile that makes you forget he's intellectually disabled, incontinent, and—except for his giggles or occasional shrieks—can't put two words together in a sentence.

I look at Greg and Ryan and try to picture the wife and mother on the scene, holding Ryan on her lap. She'd be cooing in his ear and have the banana neatly peeled and sliced in a Tupperware. And she'd wipe that banana mush from his face.

I recall that Greg is diabetic when he tosses the banana peel and reaches for his insulin kit with his free hand. Prick finger. Watch freeway. Swig sugary apple juice. Eye on Ryan. "Hey, big boy." Greg wipes his mouth and smiles at his son, who dazzles us with his grin. Greg is as driven as he drives—his hamster-wheel days seem to be filled with tackling one dizzying problem after another. Then there's his thirteen-year-old daughter, Kelsey, fascinated with her newfound appeal to boys. We won't even go there.

Sundays are the hardest. Like last week after church when Greg and the kids bumped into their mother in a drugstore. Kelsey, Ryan, and Mommy became a bundle of hugs. Greg wished he could be part of the bundle, but it was the usual awkwardness. Niceties were exchanged, and then it was time to move on. Screams and tears erupted from Ryan as they parted company. That Sunday closed out with a speeding ticket, going 50 in a 35 mph zone. He stared vacantly at the policeman. He didn't care.

The freeway still stretches in front of us, and so we drive on in silence. Finally Greg sighs, "Ryan, with those scars on his face from falling down"—he leans over and touches his son, who is a sleeping angel on the passenger seat. "I love the way he stumbles and trips his way to me whenever I come to pick him up. But . . . I don't get why God allows so much pain . . . in his life, my life. I can't bear it any longer," his voice trails. "I just don't get it."

I don't get it either, I want to say. I don't get why Greg and his ex-wife can't be a real family. Greg loves his children. When I met their mother a few weeks ago, she was as loving and caring. I want to grab them both and say, "Things aren't that bad! Love and goodness should triumph here." But it's a world of irreconcilable differences. An ex-world. Like some weird divorce between God and His world that should never have happened.

Most people live this way. I don't mean that most are divorced or the single parents of disabled kids; I mean that the situations we find ourselves in often don't get better. Problems don't always get solved. Greg and his former wife probably won't remarry. It is doubtful Ryan will experience a miracle of healing. And when life feels like nothing more than shuffling one foot in front of the other, it can shake your faith.

Most of the time we are able to manage. Like jugglers spinning plates on long sticks. And if things feel overwhelming, we try to deal with it in a heart-to-heart talk with a friend. Or we keep a journal and vent our frustrations on paper. We soak in the tub, sweat on the treadmill, splurge on a new dress, or get away to the mountains on the weekend. We smile and say we are trusting in God, but down deep we know it's a lie; we're only trusting that He doesn't load us up with more plates. But often He does.

This is what happened to Greg and his wife. Too many hurts unresolved. Too many failures at communicating. And when Ryan arrived on the scene, it made things worse. When pressures began to mount, they felt God was off somewhere tending to the needs of more obedient saints. With God feeling so distant, it choked faith out of them both.

Greg's story may be a script not unlike yours. When pain lumbers through the front door, squats down in the middle of your life, and makes itself at home day after day, year after year, it can make you choke. It can make you angry at God.

I have felt that way. When quadriplegia ambushed my life, it felt as though God were smashing me underfoot like a cigarette butt. Chronic pain on top of quadriplegia became the extra plate I could not handle, and my anger turned into deep despair. Those were nights I would thrash my head on my pillow, hoping to break it at some higher level and end my misery. Those were the mornings I refused to get out of bed; I told my sister, Jay, "Just close the drapes, turn out the light, and shut the door . . . leave me alone." Finally, after almost a year, I realized I couldn't face one more day of hope-lessness. I cried out in anguish, "God, if I can't die, *please* show me how to live."

It was the prayer God was waiting for.

THE CRY OF THE SOUL

After that, I would ask Jay to get me up, push me to the living room, and park my wheelchair in front of the music stand that held my Bible. Holding a mouth stick, I would flip this way and that, looking for answers—*any* answer. I would eventually learn—mainly through the book of Psalms—that God has His reasons. Even when it involves extra plates that make your world come crashing down. Yet our anger does not surprise or fluster Him. He knows all about it—it was God's rage that nailed the Son of God to the cross. He "gets" anger; He wrote the book on it, and He invites people—people like you and me—to come and air our grievances and complaints to Him. And the good news is you can do so without weakening your faith.

You can do so, and be all the better for it. Sound impossible? Far from it, friend. Because with the book you are holding, you have stumbled upon the *best* of guides. I should know. I first read *The Cry of the Soul* decades ago when I was still sorting through a lot of hurt and frustration connected with my quadriplegia (yes, I read it on that music stand holding a mouth stick). *The Cry of the Soul* showed me what to do with my anger and hurt—not stuff it under the carpet of my conscience, or minimize it, but actually *do* something good with it.

As I followed the Spirit's leading in chapter after chapter; as I meditated on the Scriptures, the authors' insights, and set myself on a course of action, my pain, frustration, and anger dissipated. It went away. Just like that. That's what a lively abiding in the book of Psalms can miraculously do, not to mention a fuller understanding of the character of God, as well as anger. And I owe much to Dan Allender and Tremper Longman for their take on all.

If your plates are spinning out of control—if you are crying, "God, I can't live this way!"—then please know that you have a Companion ready to step in. Comfort and consolation are about to be poured into your bruised heart. For you are safe and protected by what you will discover in *The Cry of the Soul*.

All is not lost, for your faith can and will recover. Just as my friend Greg—just as I—experienced when we made the book of Psalms our meat and drink. So make Dan Allender and Tremper Longman your friends on this journey—these gifted men are true sages when it comes to solid, practical counseling. Let them guide you; let God's Spirit guide you . . . for hope is about to break on your horizon.

Joni Eareckson Tada
Spring 2015

INTRODUCTION

When I (Dan) was ten years old, I recall visiting the "town" of a favorite TV western. I was crushed. The buildings that had looked so real on TV were, in real life, nothing but a facade with boards holding up the fake front. The empty space behind the facade pierced the illusion that the show was real. I suppose I knew it was just a show, yet nevertheless it was a shock. I never watched that show again with the same interest or enthusiasm.

The cover of this book indicates that it is about emotion. But is it simply another facade that hides the appearance of real help? "Why another book on emotions?" you might be tempted to ask. "Isn't enough enough?" We want to take you behind the cover of this book and let you see the bare boards that prop up our words—not to suggest the same effect of disillusionment and cynicism, but to invite you to consider the essential convictions that drive our writing.

Emotion is usually provoked by horizontal relational encounters. Someone treats me badly, and I feel angry or hurt. We do not differ with this assumption, but we go further: *Every emotion, though horizontally provoked, nevertheless reflects something about the vertical dimension: our relationship with God.* This book explores what our difficult emotional struggles say about our relationship with God.

And every emotion, including those we often view as negative, reveals something about the heart of God.

Here are the core convictions that structure our approach in this book.

(1) It is our conviction that emotions are not amoral—they vocalize the inner working of our souls and are as tainted as any other portion of our personality.

Many observers presume that emotions are neither right nor wrong—they simply are. Proponents of this view are concerned that once we say an emotion is right or wrong, it makes it more difficult for us to feel them honestly. Most people work hard not to feel what is unpleasant. We pretend; we deny; we distort. The concern of those who ascribe moral neutrality to emotions seems to be: if we make emotions a matter of right and wrong, then we will work that much harder to avoid feeling.

The route out of this dilemma, therefore, is to make emotions morally neutral or judgment-free. For example, a dark emotion such as anger is neither right nor wrong—it's what we do with anger that is either constructive or destructive. But this view assumes that part of our personality is free from the effects of the Fall because it presumes that our emotions escaped taint or perversion—they are essentially pure and good.

Part of understanding difficult emotions, however, is comprehending why we avoid them. The reason we don't want to feel is that feeling exposes the tragedy of our world and the darkness of our hearts. No wonder we don't want to feel: feelings expose the illusion that life is safe, good, and predictable.

The route to facing what we feel is not by devaluing the darkness of what we feel, but by valuing the deep structure of why we don't want to feel. Once we face why feeling is so hard, then we can move beyond what we feel to the deeper energy within us that keeps us from grappling honestly with our emotions. Then we will not only feel more deeply, but—more importantly—we will feel our feelings in a way that exposes our struggle with God.

One warning: Although we focus heavily on emotion, that orientation must never be considered the key to or core of growing in maturity. It is only one important element among many issues related to growing in Christlikeness—not the indispensable cornerstone to knowing God.

(2) The reason for looking inside is not to effect direct change of negative emotions to positive emotions. Instead, we are to listen to and ponder what we feel in order to be moved to the far deeper issue of what our hearts are doing with God and others.

It's foolish to assume that we can directly alter our emotions simply by willing them to change. If you're angry, it's absurd for me to say to you, "Don't be angry," and then expect that you can simply switch to feeling kind or happy.

It is also a mistake simply to work at overcoming a troublesome emotion through behavioral techniques. This is not to say that it's wrong to pray for release from rage or envy. It's inadequate, however, to assume that we can change our emotions by applying a few methods to gain handles on our troublesome inner world.

Struggling with emotions is not a matter of solving problems with a little more information and practical know-how. We are not machines that can be repaired through a series of steps—we are relational beings who are transformed by the mystery of relationship. We are radically disposed to idolatry, illusion-making, and attempts to secure our lives without bowing before God. Our core problem is not a lack of information—it is flight and rebellion.

Therefore, if we view difficult emotions as problems to be solved, we will end up looking for answers that will work rather than pursuing relationship with God, regardless of immediate outcome. A determination to resolve our emotional struggles inevitably subordinates God as a servant of our healing rather than a Person to be praised.

Rather than focusing on trying to change our emotions, we are wiser first to listen to them. They are a voice that can tell us how we are dealing with a fallen world, hurtful people, and a quizzical God who seldom seems to be or do what we expect of Him. Although emotions are generally aroused in a human context, they always reveal something about how we are dealing with God.

The revelation of reality—outside of us and within us—opens the door to wrestling with God. Encounter with God not only changes our emotions; more importantly, it has the potential to change our hearts.

It's important to realize that every emotion involves a complex interplay between body and heart. We do not merely experience anger in our minds—we feel it in our bodies. The same is true for fear, jealousy, despair, contempt, and shame. Therefore, it is dangerous to presume that all emotional struggles can be changed by a strictly "spiritual" encounter. For some, a deep spiritual encounter will include embracing biological weakness.

Certain emotions, especially anxiety and depression, involve physiological components that can often be treated with medication and other biological intervention. Ignoring the importance of the body involves a tragic misunderstanding about what it means to pursue God. It is a terrible wrong to place extra burdens on those who suffer profound emotional battles by suggesting that all they need to do is to work out their issues with God to make their struggles go away. It is equally wrong to suggest that it is unspiritual or a second-best compromise to seek physiological help. This issue is not a black-and-white, either-or option.

The biological dimension of emotion is a complex factor, which we are not ignoring. However, due to the specific approach we have taken in this book, we will not address this issue directly.

Our focus on pondering what we feel might lead some readers to conclude that we are encouraging a self-directed introspection. This is not our intention in any respect. Self-absorbed preoccupation with our inner world runs contrary to spiritual maturity. Excessive intro-spection can lead to a false sense of independence by giving us the illusion that we can exert control over our lives and become the mas-ters of our fate. This path too easily leads to arrogance or confusion.

We encourage honest inward examination for the purpose of gaining wisdom—not only to explore the question "What's going on here?" but even more, to respond to what we discover as we ask, "What am I doing with God?"

(3) Our guide for this pilgrimage of revelation is the Psalms.

Perhaps no section of Scripture more poignantly exposes the inner world of our heart and more vividly reveals the emotional life of God than the Psalms.

The Psalms were composed in poetic form. Poetry reaches to the realm beyond the world of sight and sound to reveal what our senses long to see and hear. It is the language not so much of the sublime, but of the truly real—a reality that cannot be grasped through sci-entific or theoretical precision. Theological propositions are neces-sary for understanding truth, but truth is ultimately relational, and relationship is the domain of poetry. Poetry is God's invitation to glimpse the unseen—His very character.

We focus primarily on what have been called "the psalms of dis-orientation." This type of psalm captures the struggle of the heart as the poet attempts to grasp the goodness of God in light of the heartache of life.[1] We will also allow the poetry of the Psalms to move us into the divine imagery used by the prophets, Paul, and Jesus Christ as we explore Scripture's invitation to taste the mystery of God's goodness.

(4) All emotions, including the darker ones, give us a glimpse of the character of God.

This is the heart of our book. Far more important than the way in which emotions reveal the movement of the heart is the way in which our most difficult emotions—anger, fear, jealousy, despair, contempt, and shame—uniquely reveal something about the heart of God. Our positive emotions, of course—joy, peace, pleasure, and others—have equal potential to teach us about the nature of God. But the darker struggles with emotion can point us to priceless glimpses of God's character through scriptural revelation of God's own emotions.

Oddly, so very oddly, God chooses to reveal His heart through the tainted reality of our sinful inner world. For example, He allows the psalmist to portray His anger in terms of a drunk who has just awakened with a hangover and is unleashing his rage (Psalm 78:65). What are we to learn about God through this startling picture? Does it imply that God is somehow sinful? Of course not. It implies that He reveals His heart through the multifaceted images in His Word that draw from our life experience. Language that speaks of God in what we would consider negative emotional terms reveals the mysterious humility of God: He speaks to us in ways that are sometimes shocking, disruptive, and highly charged.

Why such an apparently negative focus in this book on anger, fear, jealousy, despair, contempt, and shame? In part, it is an attempt to show these emotions as far more positive and necessary to life than we normally assume. But even more important, it is an effort to open our vision to perceive the unusual heart of God. God feels anger, fear, jealousy, despair, contempt, and shame—and all of these emotions reveal something about His character. Most gloriously, each one points to the scandalous wonder of the Cross.

The journey into our difficult emotions will reveal something about the awesome nature of the sacrifice of the eternal Son on our behalf. Ultimately, it will lead us to worship.

1

Emotions:
The Cry of the Soul

Our emotions connect our inner world to the ups and downs of life. Sometimes the connection is more than we can bear.

A woman whose husband had been fired grimaced as she told me what had happened. I asked her how she felt. Although her face began to contort in pain, she calmly stated: "I'm irritated that he was used for twenty-four years and then dropped to save on health care costs. He's fifty-four. Where is he going to find a job now? How am I going to keep him strong? It isn't fair." Her voice choked back confusion, anger, and fear.

I knew something about this woman's life. She was pleasant but determined. Her withdrawn, somewhat depressed husband did his duty each day and returned home to receive his orders for the evening. They lived a dull, conventional life that morally approximated the gospel. Now his job loss had opened the door to struggles in the marriage that they might have avoided by allowing their daily routines to distract them from the emptiness and distance in their lives.

Her grimace was the first acknowledgment that heartache was near. The heartache was over loss—job, security, prestige. But the deeper loss centered on dreams that had lain buried since the first years of their marriage. She had entered marriage with the hope that she had found a place of rest—an opportunity to let down and relax without fear. She had dreamed of the kind of intimacy that would allow her to enjoy her femininity. But gradually, those dreams were sold for the security of a stable marriage and college education for her children. Now even the payoff for her sacrifice was unraveling.

The thought crossed my mind: *She'll survive. Why open the door to anything more?* If she opened her heart to feel, she would battle with far more than finances. She would face her decaying marriage. She would grapple with questions she never had the courage to ask about her husband, herself, and God.

RIDING THE UPS AND DOWNS OF EMOTION

Emotion links our internal and external worlds. To be aware of what we feel can open us to questions we would rather ignore. For many of us, that is precisely why it is easier not to feel. But a failure to feel leaves us barren and distant from God and others. We often seem caught between extremes of feeling too much or not enough.

Emotions are like the wind—full of mystery. They come and go suddenly, often leaving havoc and debris in their wake. Our destructive feelings, in particular, can seem like independent, capricious forces that are confusing and out of control. A mature, professional woman recently told me,

Everyone who knows me would say I am stable, in control, and happy. Normally, I am. But every now and then some insignificant event will trigger a torrent of rage that is not only excessive, but irrational. Other times when I hear a friend is going through a tough time I feel so sad that it can haunt me for days. I know the words *torrent* and *haunt* are strong. I don't feel that way often, but when I do there are no other words to describe my feelings.

Emotions seem to be one of the least reliable yet most influential forces that guide our lives. Some days we feel great. Confidence and good tidings glide us into the new day; we tackle difficult tasks and succeed. Other days we might experience a downswing in emotion that we can't explain and are helpless to change.

We spend a great deal of energy trying to ride the crest above the churning undertow of emotion. What are we to do with the ups and downs of emotion? Why do we either ignore our feelings or battle them off as if they were an enemy?

WHY EMOTIONS CAN BE SO DIFFICULT

One explanation for why we avoid our feelings is that it's painful to feel. To feel hurt, hurts. To feel shame, shames. To feel any loss only intensifies sorrow. In one sense, that's true. But then why do we try to avoid *good* feelings? One woman told me that she always feels a slight dread whenever she begins to feel hope.

Perhaps a better explanation for why it's so difficult to feel our feelings is that *all* emotion, positive or negative, opens the door to the nature of reality. All of us prefer to avoid pain—but even more, we want to escape reality.

Even when life is delightful, joy is fleeting and its brief appearance only deepens our desire for more. Pleasure holds a wistful incompleteness because, even at best, it is a poor picture of what we were meant to enjoy. As a result, we never feel completely satisfied with our present life, no matter how well things go. Anticipation inevitably carries with it disappointment and longing.

Emotion propels us into the tragic recognition that we are not home. And if this is true of our most pleasurable moments, then isn't it even more true of our painful memories and experiences?

We will never fully enjoy what we were meant to experience until heaven. But it is not easy to embrace the tragedy of the Fall and our distance from home. Paul describes this recognition as an inward "groaning," equating it with the agony of a woman giving birth:

> We know that the whole creation has been groaning as in the pains of childbirth right up to the present time. Not only so, but we ourselves, who have the firstfruits of the Spirit, groan inwardly as we wait eagerly for our adoption to sonship, the redemption of our bodies.
> *Romans 8:22-23*

At this moment, the whole earth is caught in the agony of childbirth. In one form or another, we are all groaning in anticipation. Yet we are often numb to the anguish.

Consider the pain of one of my clients. Her husband was an elder in their church, an avid reader of theological works, a committed believer, and an all-around good family man. But one day, after nearly twenty years of marriage, he came home and announced he was leaving her. "I have never been happy," he declared. "I have never done anything just for me. I am tired of feeling like a hypocrite. I have met a woman who makes me glad to be alive. I am sorry to hurt you, but I am going to live for the first time in my life."

I talk to many people in pain, but this woman's face haunts me. She wanted help and answers more desperately than she wanted to live. But although her heart was heaving in grief, her words were hollow and numb. She was impervious to any hope that might open her to more pain. She didn't want to embrace the anguish of reality. She wanted to know what she could do to become a woman who would make her husband happy to be alive.

The pains of life in a fallen world turn us into something not fully human. When we experience pain, our deepest passion is to escape the bludgeons of assault, betrayal, and loss. Most of us don't resort to the deadness that buffered my client's pain. But in our desperation, each of us in our own way tries to dull the intensity of our groaning.

We might cling to emotional responses that enable us to cope with the harm that comes in small and large doses. For example, many men find it easier to feel anger than hurt. And many women find it safer to feel hurt or confusion rather than anger. So we buttress our sagging confidence and relieve our ambivalence by resorting to anger. We justify our flight through confusion and fear. We escape sadness by opting for shame; we bypass loss by giving in to jealousy. In other words, we use one emotion to hide from other, more painful feelings.

Another way to dull the intensity of our inward groaning is by attempting to avoid our emotions. For many, strong feelings are an infrequent, foreign experience. Their inner life is characterized by an inner coolness, bordering on indifference. Unfortunately, this is often mistaken for trust. In many circles, passionate emotions are discouraged as unspiritual. You are considered godly if you can handle difficult trials with a detached and apparently unruffled confidence.

But this conclusion is wrong. There are times when lack of emotion is simply the by-product of hardness and arrogance. The Scriptures reveal that this absence of feelings is often a refusal to face the sorrow of life and the hunger for heaven; it is not the mark of maturity, but rather the boast of evil (see Isaiah 47:8; Revelation 18:7).

Our refusal to embrace our emotions is often an attempt to escape the agony of childbirth and buttress the illusion of a safe world. It is an attempt to deal with a God who does not relieve our pain.

The presence of disruptive emotions that feel irrational or out of control is not necessarily a sign of disease, sin, or trauma. Instead, it may be the signal that the heart is struggling with God. Therefore, we must view the ups and downs of our emotional life not as a problem to be resolved, but as a cry to be heard.

LISTENING TO OUR EMOTIONS

Emotions open the door to asking hard questions: Does life make sense? Is there any real purpose to my pain? Why must every relationship end? Is God good? If we are to understand ourselves honestly—and, more importantly, know God—we must listen to our emotions.

But the voices are legion that counsel, "Ignore what you feel. It will only get you into deeper trouble. Just get control, repent of negative feelings, believe by faith, choose the right course of action, and trust that emotions will follow like an obedient caboose." Are those voices right? Is it a question of taming our emotional struggles and trying to do what's right, day by day?

The Bible reveals that our inner world is complex. By God's design we are complicated creatures. And further, we are deceitfully convoluted because of depravity. Through divine inspiration Jeremiah warns: "The heart is deceitful above all things and beyond cure. Who can understand it?" (Jeremiah 17:9). Clearly, handling our inner world is more complex than simply making a choice to manage our emotions.

The psalmist calls us to ponder our inner world, not neglect it: "Why, my soul, are you downcast?" he repeatedly asks. (See Psalm 42:11.) Ignoring our emotions is turning our back on reality; listening to our emotions ushers us into reality. And reality is where we meet God.

If we want to know God, we must ponder and struggle with our feelings to gain an understanding of the passions that rule us. Nothing illuminates the ruling passions of our heart as dramatically or clearly as our emotions. And no book of Scripture illuminates our emotions as dramatically or clearly as the Psalms. In the next chapter, we will see how the Psalms provide a voice for us to bring the cry of our soul before God.

EMOTIONS REVEAL HOW WE'RE DOING WITH GOD

What are we to listen for in our emotions? The answer is, in part: *We are to listen for the direction of our heart.* The question, *What do I feel?* is in fact another way of asking, *Who am I? What direction am I moving in?*

We most often think of emotions in horizontal terms—how we're doing in relation to people in our lives. But in a deeper sense, emotions reveal what's happening on a vertical level. They provide a window on the question, *What am I doing with God?*

The heart's movement can be calibrated and assessed in light of many different criteria, but all evaluations eventually boil down to this: *Am I moving toward God or away from Him?* Am I turning toward God with awe and gratitude, or away from Him toward false gods of my own making?

Emotions are the language of the soul. They are the cry that gives the heart a voice. To understand our deepest passions and convictions, we must learn to listen to the cry of the soul.

However, we often turn a deaf ear—through emotional denial, distortion, or disengagement. We strain out anything disturbing in order to gain tenuous control of our inner world. We are frightened and ashamed of what leaks into our consciousness. In neglecting our intense emotions, we are false to ourselves and lose a wonderful opportunity to know God. We forget that change comes through brutal honesty and vulnerability before God. Only face to face with our deepest ruling passions is there hope of redeeming the fabric of our inner world.

Listening is the first step toward altering destructive emotions. Are you pursuing God? Your emotions will tell you. Are you pursuing false gods? Your emotional life will provide strong clues to the nature of your soul's direction.

But how? Are we to presume that good feelings are the sign of faithful pursuit of God, and bad feelings the sign of idolatry? How easy if it were that simple. We can't slap labels on our emotions as positive or negative, good or bad. Neither can we "fix" our emotional struggles as if they were so many broken toys.

We can, however, view our emotions from the perspective of whether they lead us to engagement with God or move us away from greater dependence on Him. We can listen to what they tell us about our struggles. Emotions are like messengers from the front lines of the battle zone. Our tendency is to kill the messenger. But if we listen carefully, we will learn how to fight the war successfully.

Listening to our emotions requires that we know how to speak the language of the heart. That is what we will be doing in the rest of this book: learning to speak the language of the heart by discovering how our emotions, particularly the difficult ones, reveal our deepest questions about God. And, ultimately, we will discover how these flawed emotions can give us unique and priceless glimpses of the character of God.

Emotion is a difficult topic. If you picked up this book because you wanted to discover how to find tranquility and ease amid the uncertainties of life, you will be disappointed. Peace that passes all understanding is possible, but more often than not it is an occasional refuge that comes only after wrestling with the inner realities of our struggles with life and with God.

Therefore, don't assume that resolving your turbulent emotions is the key to meeting God. It is actually within the inner mayhem of life that a stage is built for the intrusive story of His light and hope. The absence of tumult, more than its presence, is an enemy of the soul.

God meets you in your weakness, not in your strength. He comforts those who mourn, not those who live above desperation. He reveals Himself more often in darkness than in the happy moments of life.

This book outlines a journey that exposes the deepest questions of the heart. You won't discover the kinds of answers that alleviate struggle. But you can encounter a person, God Himself, who exults in using darkness to reveal the brilliance of His infinite goodness. In hope that you will meet God, we ask you to choose to plunge into the emotions of anger, fear, jealousy, despair, contempt, and shame that yearn to be transformed.

2

The Psalms:
The Voice of the Soul

The event took place during the early, crazy hours of a dark morning in a hotel room, while I was away from my family. Awakened at three because my joints ached, I could not fall back to sleep. My emotions began racing with a vague sense of terror.

At first I had no idea how to make sense of the emotional turbulence that eventually carried me to denial. I tried to shut out the growing horror by lying in bed and letting idle thoughts roll me away from the turmoil. I remained detached from my physical pain and growing dread until I remembered these words from Psalm 77:

> I cried out to God for help;
>   I cried out to God to hear me.
> When I was in distress, I sought the Lord;
>   at night I stretched out untiring hands,
>   and I would not be comforted.

> I remembered you, God, and I groaned;
>
> I meditated, and my spirit grew faint.
>
> *Psalm 77:1-3*

The words tugged at my heart. In my desire to run from the disquiet, I was settling for easy answers. The psalmist meditated and grew faint. I dabbled with reality and grew hard. The psalmist invited me to struggle, to flesh out my complaint before God in order to grasp something about His character. I was compelled to voice what I would have preferred to keep silent.

Since I could neither sleep nor endure my flight into denial, I started to write.

It is early in the morning, and my joints ache. The bed is damp from fear as I look into my future. I am awake but I am trying to convince myself that I will quickly fall back to sleep.

The terror that has descended seems magnified in the darkness of a foreign bed. My night terror is the looming specter of crippling arthritis. I am forty years old and already my neck cracks with the dead sounds of a dry limb. My hands ache, and I cannot grip the sheets to move to a new position without pain.

As I look ahead, the vision of horror plays out in the darkened and lonely theater of my imagination. I am going to be crippled, confined to an earthly hell, while my family and friends go skiing, play tennis, or stroll along a well-lit street in downtown Denver on the way to a delicious Italian meal. I am a crustacean, a distant memory that provokes sadness, a burden that engenders pity and labored patience.

I feel loneliness, then fury. How can this happen? My fury glides into envy. Then I round the corner into stark, naked terror. All in the span of minutes, my emotions race like a wind through an open window, blowing every unfastened paper into a chaotic debris.

"What do You want from me, God? Will You gain greater glory through my crippling? I will not survive, unless I know something more about Your purpose. What must I comprehend to understand You?"

My heart was spent. After writing that last sentence, I eventually fell back to sleep.

Emotions are the cry of the soul. They expose what we are doing with the sorrow of life and in turn reveal what our heart is doing with God.

Emotions, like fear, give us a glimpse of the stark demands we make on God that we are usually ignorant of or willfully reluctant to face. The intense fear I experienced that night, brought on by visions of debilitating arthritis, exposed what was going on inside me. Underneath, I was demanding that God take away my fear, remove my pain, and provide a reasonably pleasant life. His unwillingness to comply with my demands pushed aside the thin veneer of busyness that coats the surface of my status-quo life. I was left helpless before Him.

THE NEED FOR A DISRUPTING VOICE

How do we quiet our hearts long enough to listen to our tumultuous emotions? We can start by hearing the divinely inspired words of those who provide us with glimpses into their inner worlds. No section of the Bible teaches us the language of the soul better than the Psalms, which reflect the movement of the human heart in rich, evocative, and startling language. In a voice that disrupts, invites, and reveals, the psalmist draws us to the voice of God.

The Psalms teach us how to praise and worship. But they also teach us how to wrestle with doubt until it gives way to the first rays of hope. The Psalms light our way on the path of change.

Writers and thinkers throughout the Christian tradition have recognized the soul-exposing function of this pivotal book of the Bible. John Calvin offered this brilliant insight:

> What various and resplendent riches are contained in this treasury, it were difficult to describe. . . . I have been wont to call this book, not inappropriately, an anatomy of all parts of the soul; for there is not an emotion of which any one can be conscious that is not here represented as in a mirror.[1]

The Psalms mirror the human soul. We look into them, and we see ourselves.

A Voice That Disrupts Our Denial

The Psalms provoke us to move out of denial. Christians are particularly adept at numbing themselves against painful emotions. "After all," we reason, "we should be joyful because we know that God is in control." Negative emotions such as fear, anger, or depression are stigmatized as inappropriate because God is love and grants us peace.

But our spiritual songbook of Psalms does not contain 150 hymns of joy. As a matter of fact, a close look shows that the psalms of complaint and songs of accusation—the music of confusion, doubt, and heartache—significantly outnumber the hymns of joy. We may seek to flee from the feelings inside of us, but a look into the Psalms exposes them to our gaze. Calvin described this exposure:

> [The psalmists] lay open their inmost thoughts and affections [emotions], call, or rather draw, each of us to the examination

of himself in particular, in order that none of the many infirmities to which we are subject, and of the many vices with which we abound, may remain concealed.[2]

The psalmist's ruthless honesty compels us to look beyond the surface of our tumult, deeper into our soul, where we expose our battle with God. As the psalmist cries "out of the depths" (Psalm 130:1), we find ourselves crying out to God along with him.

The Psalms disrupt our assumption that we can escape the "groaning" of this life. They call us back from our natural tendency to flee from pain and fight against any who provoke discomfort. They expose the essence of our emotional turmoil—the commitment to find life apart from trusting God.

A Voice That Disrupts Our Depravity

Our culture presumes that emotions are amoral—neither right nor wrong. According to this perspective, it's not what we *feel* that's potentially sinful, but rather what we *do* with our feelings. The problem with this view is its assumption that some element of our personality escaped the consequences of the Fall.

It seems more accurate to say that our feelings are not any more or less sinful than our thoughts, desires, and behaviors. But God can use our emotions to disclose sin through revealing the depths of our battle with Him.

The Psalms expose the sinfulness of our anger, fear, jealousy, despair, contempt, and shame. Notice how envy exposed the psalmist's inner disease:

Surely God is good to Israel,
    to those who are pure in heart.
But as for me, my feet had almost slipped;
    I had nearly lost my foothold.

THE CRY OF THE SOUL

> For I envied the arrogant
>> when I saw the prosperity of the wicked.
>
> *Psalm 73:1-3*

The psalmist's jealousy reveals his sinful desire for the rewards of the wicked, but it does more—it exposes his sense of futility in remaining pure. Why be pure when God seems to give the blessings of life to the wicked and not to the righteous?

From our limited perspective, emotions seem to spring from horizontal cause-and-effect. Someone is unkind to me; I feel hurt or angry. Another person is kind; I feel happy. My colleague receives an award; I feel jealous. Feelings seem to follow the ups and downs of relating to others—they don't, at first glance, seem to have much to do with God.

A friend once told me (Dan): "I feel like I'm part of a cosmic, county fair bumper-car ride. I know I'm going to get hit; it's only a matter of when and how hard." I asked him if his sense of dread was related to God. "Not really," he replied. "I just wonder when things are going to collapse, or when I'm going to get knocked down again."

But all dread is related to the question, *Is life predictable?* All anger is related to the question, *Is life just?* Change the word "life" to "God," and the questions become personal. *Is God predictable? Is God just?* The psalmist's jealousy surfaced in the horizontal context of human circumstances, but it was rooted in his underlying question, *Is God fair?*

The Psalms help us understand that *every emotion is a theological statement.* All feelings reveal our attempt to maneuver into a position of regaining access to the pleasures and perfection of God. All dark emotions are rooted in our *reactive* response (flight) to being out of the Garden and our *aggressive* response (fight) to regain access to Eden.

Our natural response to pain is the attempt to get relief from our suffering—either by fighting in anger or fleeing in fear. When we're angry, we naturally attack or threaten assault if the perceived unjust offense continues. When we're afraid, flight seems like the most reasonable course in the world.

Notice what these people of God do when they feel the pain of hunger: "Distressed and hungry, they will roam through the land; when they are famished, they will become enraged and, looking upward, will curse their king and their God" (Isaiah 8:21).

Unrighteous anger demands that others respond to our plight or pay the consequences. Ultimately, when we are empty and God does not respond as we wish, we feel justified to act on our own behalf. And we turn our rage against Him because He *could* alleviate our suffering.

The psalmist disrupts our denial that we are angry or afraid. He disrupts our pretense that our anger and fear are not directed against God. "The problem is not the situation that provoked your fear and anger," he tells us. "The problem is that your heart is opposed to God."

Yet even as he exposes the depths of our hearts, the psalmist does something quite odd—he invites us to question, doubt, and rage against God.

THE NEED FOR AN INVITING VOICE

A client told me a tragic story about her violent father, who beat her often. After one occasion he solicitously said to her, "I know you hate me. Tell me what you feel after I spank you."

She was leery, but his voice was tender and his eyes were kind. "Tell me, honey. I want to know if things between us are okay."

After much resistance, she finally whispered, "I hate you." Her father then beat her twice as severely as before.

We fear the same may be true with God. We shudder with dread that we will suffer terrible consequences for our inner rebellion.

Precisely at this point, the Psalms surprise us. They not only help us articulate and understand what we feel, but they also dare us to struggle. Even more, they give us the words to vocalize our desperate struggles with the Lord.

The psalmists felt, and publicly expressed, the gamut of emotions—from hurt to fury, from desire for vengeance to contempt against God. How comforting to know that we are not alone when we ache with loneliness, burn with anger, and tremble with fear. Someone before us has faced these emotions and, in the midst of that conflict, learned to love God.

A Voice That Invites Us to Hurt

The psalmist is not afraid to speak his heart to God. Unwilling to hide behind trite spiritual platitudes, he declares:

> I am worn out from my groaning.
> All night long I flood my bed with weeping
>   and drench my couch with tears.
> My eyes grow weak with sorrow;
>   they fail because of all my foes.
> *Psalm 6:6-7*

In this declaration, the pain of life is not spiritualized away or tempered by trite steps to get a handle on personal agony—it is entered into and vocalized with passion. We are invited to enter the pain of our hurt without apology or compromise.

A Voice That Invites Us to Rage

The psalmist brings his struggle to God and, at times, accuses Him of being faithless—even a lousy businessman. "You gave us up to be devoured like sheep and have scattered us among the nations," he scolds God. "You sold your people for a pittance, gaining nothing from their sale" (44:11-12). He wags his finger at God's face, accusing Him not only of negligence, but idiocy.

Elsewhere the psalmist furiously mocks God for bringing pain into his life:

You have taken from me my closest friends
    and have made me repulsive to them.
I am confined and cannot escape;
    my eyes are dim with grief.
I call to you, LORD, every day;
    I spread out my hands to you.
Do you show your wonders to the dead?
    Do their spirits rise up and praise you?
Is your love declared in the grave,
    your faithfulness in Destruction?

Psalm 88:8-11

Some believers cringe from this language of desperation and rage, even though they have the model of the psalmist. "The psalmist didn't have Christ, but we do—so we can't be lonely, angry, or afraid!"

But this is presumption, not faith. The laments of the Psalms encourage us to risk the danger of speaking boldly and personally to the Lord of the universe.

Walter Brueggemann reminds us that "the laments are refusals to settle for the way things are. They are acts of relentless hope that believes no situation falls outside Yahweh's capacity for transformation. No situation falls outside of Yahweh's responsibility."[3]

The Psalms do not offer an analytical treatment of emotions. They are not a how-to text from which we can extrapolate four easy steps to resolving difficult emotions. Such simplistic reductions of our inner world, and of life itself, strip the heart of calling out to God in the darkness of His mysterious involvement with us.

Instead, the Psalms invite us to question God. But they do this in the context of worship—they were the hymnal used in public worship. God invites us to bring before Him our rage, doubt, and terror—but He intends for us to do so as part of worship. This is the kind of emotional struggle we must engage in if we are to fathom the nature of God's heart for us.

THE NEED FOR A REVEALING VOICE

What can we expect from God? What is He really like? What will He do with us once our denial and sin are disrupted and our hurt and fury drawn forth?

It is in the dark struggles with God that we are surprised by His response to our anger and fear. What we receive from Him during our difficult battle is not what we expect. We assume He wants order, conformity—obedient children. Instead, we find that He wants our passionate involvement and utter awe in the mystery of His glorious character.

A Voice That Reveals God's Heart for Us

The Psalms disclose God's fiery love for His people. He draws us to the extreme edge of life, where we cannot live by careful, well-planned control. This is where the desert begins. It is where darkness draws us to a realm of desperation and dependence. It is the place where trust can grow. God's passion is to rig the world so that we are compelled to deal with whatever blocks us from being like His glorious Son.

The psalmist marvels that he can't fake God out. Wherever he runs, God is already there:

You know when I sit and when I rise;
　　you perceive my thoughts from afar. . . .

Where can I go from your Spirit?
    Where can I flee from your presence? . . .
If I rise on the wings of the dawn,
    if I settle on the far side of the sea,
even there your hand will guide me,
    your right hand will hold me fast.
If I say, "Surely the darkness will hide me
    and the light become night around me,"
even the darkness will not be dark to you;
    the night will shine like the day,
    for darkness is as light to you.

Psalm 139:2, 7, 9-12

Wherever we flee, there God is—to express His love for us and reveal our unique role for His purpose. The Psalms reveal that God is slow to anger, rich in mercy, and long-suffering in grace. His purposes for us are good.

In the darkness of our emotional wrestling with God, we grow in our understanding of Him. When He does not respond to us as we expect, we learn about His surprising character. We attack Him with anger, but we do not receive His judgment in return. We plead desperately for Him to save us from terror, but He does not necessarily rescue us with immediate resolution of our circumstances. However, what He does reveal is His heart for us.

Further, our darkest emotions reveal something—though in a skewed, bent, and tarnished way—about God's emotional life. How can we begin to understand the nature of God's anger unless we enter into our own? How are we to gain any picture of what it means for a holy, righteous God to be jealous for His people if we ignore our human envy and jealousy? In the most peculiar fashion, He chooses to reveal His perfect heart by analogy with human emotion that is stained by depravity. If we are to comprehend more richly the heart of God, it is imperative that we seek to understand our internal world.

The Psalms propel us into the deepest questions about ourselves, about others, and about God. As we let them expose the depths of our emotion, they will lead us to the God who reveals Himself in the midst of our struggle.

3
—
Relationships:
The Context of the Cry

Emily lay in a hospital bed, the captive of tubes and machines humming quietly as she fought for her life. Just two days earlier she had kissed her husband, run out to second base, and crouched for the first pitch of a church softball league. Before the pitch came, she fell to her knees and collapsed.

After being rushed to a local hospital, Emily was transferred to the ICU of a large city hospital. She had suffered an aneurysm. For hours, she hung between life and death as she underwent surgery.

The doctors cut open her skull and lifted her brain to gain access to the two clots that imperiled her life. They removed the clots. But today Emily remains in a coma, her life hanging in the balance. If she lives, she may be severely crippled.

Just a week before Emily's collapse, I (Dan) had spent an hour with these good friends. We laughed and talked about the odd, wonderful work of God. Emily is a spirited, creative, loving woman whose life has prompted me to pray for greater courage and kindness in my own life. Just the other day she was asking me several questions about how I handle pain; now she lingers in a drug-induced coma, waiting on God to decrease the swelling in her brain or to take her to a place where there is no agony.

"HOW LONG, O LORD?"

After the tragedy I sat with Emily's husband, tears filling my eyes. As my sorrow increased, so did my anger. "How long, O Lord?" I railed. "How long can You bear to see the skulls of Your loved ones cut open? How long can You see the tears of scared children as they cry themselves to sleep, wondering if their mother will be alive when they awake? How long, O Lord?"

The cry of the soul is the suffering of childbirth, the anguished waiting for God to redeem our bodies and souls, the heavens and the earth. The complaint of the soul, "How long?" is a plea, a prayer, an accusation.

Every person lives a unique story, composed of moments of great joy and tragic pain. Each moment of pleasure and pain compels us to ask uniquely personal questions: "Why did my dad abuse me? . . . Why did my mom die before I had a chance to know her? . . . What is God's purpose in giving me musical gifts? . . . What am I to do with the wealth of my family?" But every personal question reflects a far deeper, existential struggle: "What is the nature of life? And who or what is God?" Consequently, although our emotions are provoked by the various individual themes of our story, they all echo a common question: "Is God good?"

My friend, Emily's husband, spoke about his suffering and heartache with passion and faith. He also spoke about God in ways that did not deny the struggle. He had been gripped by the force of life and death, the pain of God and a passionate, visionary hope.

But as he told me about his suffering and his hope in God, I felt contempt for him. Contempt was certainly not what I wanted or expected to feel. I respect my friend, but that night I felt a growing desire to speak to him realistically, even harshly. Didn't he realize his wife might die?

Why would I feel contempt toward a good friend as he offered me a taste of God's goodness in his life? Looking back, I believe it is because I envied his faith. I don't want to go through what he has suffered. Yet he has glimpsed the face of God and has seen His mercy in the midst of sorrow.

His life moved toward me with the offer of knowing God better. In response, I flinched. I tried to dull the desire to know God with such deep passion. My contempt blocked God's invitation to trust Him in the face of sorrow.

My angry question, "Why don't You do something, God?" was an aggressive reaction: to fight in order to avoid desire and trust. It seemed unfair for God to ask me simultaneously to want Emily to be healed while trusting Him no matter what He chose to do.

I fought God's movement toward me. Then, in contempt, I fled from it. I wasn't simply fleeing from my friend, or from pain or confusion. Ultimately, my contempt was flight from God.

All our emotions find their final object of focus in Him. I say this because at the root of all joy is the wonder of redemption; at the core of all difficult emotion is the question, "God, are You good?"

King David points toward God as the ultimate Being against whom we sin and struggle: "Against you, you only, have I sinned and done what is evil in your sight; so you are right in your verdict and justified when you judge" (Psalm 51:4).

Our emotional struggles reflect far more than our battle with people and events; they reveal our deepest questions about God. But how do we make the connection from the horizontal circumstances that provoke our emotions to the vertical conditions they point to?

In this chapter, we will explore three fundamental types of relational movement (against, away, and toward) that provoke our emotions. This context helps clarify how our responses in human relationships are rooted in the nature of our relationship with God. As we understand what situationally provokes our emotions, we will open the door to recognizing the deeper struggles involved in all emotion.

WHAT PROVOKES OUR FEELINGS?

Although feelings often seem unpredictable and irrational, they are neither random nor unprovoked. True, different people react differently to different situations, but due to our common heritage as persons made in the image of God, we share some predictable patterns.

Our emotions are based on our responses to how others deal with us. Our feelings are provoked when people relate to us in one of three ways: (1) they move against us: *attack*; (2) they move away from us: *abandonment*; (3) they move toward us: *love*. In the context of a sinful, fallen world, our emotional responses to these relational movements can generally be characterized as *fight* or *flight*. The following diagram shows how these responses give rise to our difficult emotions.

Relational Movement	Fight Response	Flight Response
Attack (against)	Anger	Fear
Abandonment (away)	Jealousy	Despair
Love (toward)	Contempt	Shame

There are factors involved in what prompts us to choose the option of fight or flight. Our life stories will shape which basic attitude, fight or flight, is more deeply imbedded in our responses to others. Obviously, specific situations will also provide clues as to which response is more naturally chosen.

What is our emotional reaction when someone attacks us? We either return the attack in anger or retreat in fear. How do we respond to the loss of abandonment? We either cling desperately in a jealous rage or withdraw from the pain of involvement in despair. How do we feel when someone loves us but we view that love as too disruptive and dangerous? We fight off our need for it with skepticism and contempt or flee from the need it exposes in us by withdrawing in shame.

Each relational movement provokes a consequent emotional response in us. These responses open the door to our deeper questions about God.

ATTACK: THE VIOLATION OF OUR DIGNITY

An attack provokes us to fight (anger) or flight (fear). An assault by a friend complicates the normal response of fear or anger by adding shock and disappointment.

When someone attacks us, they threaten us with destruction—of our position, property, person, or power. At the very least, they want to keep us from enjoying what we have. Relational assaults can be unrelenting, crafty, deceitful, and subtle—and are almost always a surprise.

Sometimes the attacks we experience are so subtle that we ignore their cumulative effect. But our emotional response is likely to be a movement between anger and fear.

Anger revolves around the question, *Is God just—will He let the wicked win?* Fear centers on the question, *Will God protect me?*

Anger: Fighting Fire with Fire

When we respond to an assault with our own attack, we are fighting fire with fire. Anger propels us into the battle. It is a response to a perceived or actual injustice that attempts to destroy the wrong done to us. Whether righteous or unrighteous, anger triggers activity: Our breathing quickens, muscles tighten, eyes narrow and focus on the enemy. Anger spurs immediate and decisive choice.

One man remarked, "I usually don't make a decision until I get myself upset. If I'm calm and reasoned, then I can see both sides of my choice and I don't know what to do. But once I get a little angry, then I can make a choice without caring what other people think." Many of us make choices with an internal chip on our shoulder. Anger is an adrenaline that increases our courage to move in a world that seems to oppose our desire.

Unrighteous anger dulls the pain of desperation and aggressively demands justice; since God fails to protect us, we are justified in taking matters into our own hands. Anger vocalizes the core question, *Is God just—will He let the wicked win and prevail against me?*

Anger attempts to rectify God's passivity by empowering us to act instead of waiting vulnerably for God to do something. It is not only a protection against harm and an energizer for battle; it is a taunt against God for apparently refusing to act on our behalf.

Fear: Anger in Reverse

When confronted with harm that can overpower us, fear energizes us to flee. It quickens our retreat. It makes any movement forward into battle seem absurd.

Fear triggers a dilation of the pupils, as if our eyes are opening wide enough to take in all the data necessary to avoid destruction. Our stomach tightens, heaviness descends, and sweat glands release moisture to "cool" down the physical machine so that it doesn't burn up. The body is prepared for flight and hiding. As fear increases, the body is prepared to shut down and curl up. At its extreme, terror is immobilizing.

In order to preserve ourselves, we will do whatever seems reasonable to escape. The anxiety demands that for our own survival, we back away from the threatening person or problem.

Both fear and anger are self-justifying; fear simply moves us in the opposite direction of anger. Ungodly fear dulls the pain of desperation and passively demands protection; since God fails to protect me, I am justified to act on my own behalf. Fear vocalizes the core question, *Can I trust God to protect me from harm?*

ABANDONMENT: THE WITHDRAWAL OF INTIMACY

Abandonment inevitably leads to loss: the loneliness of living in isolation from those who mean the most to us. It is separation, but it feels like death: It signals the end of relationship.

Every human relationship is haunted by potential abandonment. Our friends could betray us, our children spurn us, our spouse divorce us. Abandonment invades every relationship and mocks intimacy.

Loss is a cruel taunt. It deepens desire as it takes away hope. Loss and abandonment provoke jealousy (fight) and despair (flight). Jealousy asks the question, *Is God good, or will He leave me empty and bless others?* Despair asks, *Will God leave me isolated and alone?*

Jealousy: Possessive Rage

Jealousy comes from wanting to keep what we angrily fear we might lose; envy comes from wanting to gain what we do not have. Both jealousy and envy involve a furious demand that our soul not suffer loss.

One man complained, "How dare my wife smile and talk and actually touch the arm of another man? She spoke to our pastor as if she were his mistress." His jealousy was making him physically sick—green with desire.

Jealousy builds a fence around the one who might leave; it is a possessive rage that attempts to protect the beloved from a rival suitor and the self from loss.

Envy also works to escape loss. It is painful to see another enjoy what we lack, so we become thieves who ransack or steal the pleasures of others. Rather than bear the loss and trust in God's goodness, we strike out against those who seem to threaten or enjoy what we desperately claim as our own.

James tells us that our envious fury becomes murderous when we suffer the loss of what we desire: "You desire but do not have, so you kill. You covet but you cannot get what you want, so you quarrel and fight" (James 4:2). Ungodly jealousy dulls the pain of loss and aggressively demands satisfaction; since God fails to provide for me, I am justified to act on my own behalf. Jealousy vocalizes the core question, *Is God good—will He satisfy my hunger? Or will He bless others and leave me empty?*

Despair: Flight from Loneliness

Despair is the refusal to struggle. It deadens our heart to the hope that we will be rescued, redeemed, and happy.

A friend spoke of her crumbling marriage: "I cannot bear the thought that my husband might change. I have hoped for years that he would be the man I know he could be, but I grew so weary of the ups and downs of disappointment that I have given up desiring for him to change. I hate hope. I refuse to want something again, only to be as devastated as I have been all these years." Despair refuses to hope.

Proverbs declares, "Hope deferred makes the heart sick, but a longing fulfilled is a tree of life" (13:12). A better translation of the word "sick" is *nausea*. "Sick" implies not feeling well; nausea is overwhelming. If hope deferred makes the soul sick, then it's no wonder most of us spend our lives in denial, focusing our passions on more trivial desires. Such despair saves us from the possibility of really wanting something that might be denied us.

We hate to be lonely. We might enjoy being alone, but we despise being cut off and isolated from others. We desire intimacy, yet despair deadens our sense of caring whether anyone wants relationship with us. It allows us to wallow in our failures rather than face our need.

Ungodly despair dulls the loneliness and passively demands some kind of relief; since God fails to offer His presence for comfort, I am justified to act on my own behalf. Despair vocalizes the core question, *Is God good, or will He leave me in isolation? Will He offer His presence to others and leave me alone?*

Living with an inner dullness works for a while. However, life— or, more accurately, God—refuses to allow us to exist as robots. Suffering strips us of that strategy by forcing us either to struggle with God or to kill our desires—in essence, to commit soul murder. God provokes us to move out of our complacency and mediocrity by moving toward us, arousing our deepest passions.

LOVE: THE PURSUIT OF OUR HEARTS

Despair dulls us to any movement made toward us that might arouse the desire for intimacy. The repeated cycle of desire aroused, hope disappointed, and soul deadened through despair leads to a hatred of desire.

Desire is an enemy that can be neutralized through contempt. Contempt is our means of fighting against the arousal of hope when someone moves toward us, offering kindness and tenderness. If hope penetrates the facade of contempt, we often feel like fools who have been set up and used. Shame comes when our desire for intimacy exposes us as naked and needy. Therefore, the offer of intimacy often provokes contempt (fight) or shame (flight).

Intimacy is a taste of reconciliation. It is a testimony to the fact that separation and loss have been overcome. Moments of connection reflect our hunger for redemption, for perfect relationship with God. Although we crave redemption, we are also reluctant to let our desires exceed our control. We work hard to dull the potential for assault or loss that comes when we open our hearts to intimacy.

However, God will not leave us in our superficiality or sullen despair. Nor will He allow our puny shields of anger to stall Him. He will not leave us alone. He pursues. He intrudes. He will use any and every means to do so. He constantly moves toward us, arousing both desire and ambivalence. We want and we don't want the grace that can break our hearts. We know that involvement with God will require the removal of our deepest defenses. He never merely takes us as we are. He receives us and changes us. We want change, and we do not want change.

C. S. Lewis pictures this battle in the memorable character of Eustace in *The Voyage of the Dawn Treader*. Eustace succumbed to the powers of evil and was turned into a dragon. He could return to being a human only if he was willing to let Aslan (the Christ figure) cut him open with his sharp claws. To Eustace, this was insanity: He would perish! Yet that was the whole point. His life depended on his willingness to die. He hated his condition and wanted change, but he was terrified to die. His ambivalence tore him to pieces.

So does ours. We fight God's movement toward us and relieve our ambivalence with contempt and shame. Here, the deepest difficulties of the human heart come to the surface. The questions *Is God just? Is He good?* become more simple and personal: *Does God love me?*

Contempt: The Shield of Mockery

Contempt smells kindness, grace, and compassion and turns up its nose in disgust.

We desperately want love, but passion seems dangerous. Consequently, we shun loving movement toward us by treating it with contempt. We're really asking, *If you move toward me, I will be aroused with the anticipation of involvement. But what if you don't really want me? What if your movement toward me is really meant for another, or—worse—meant for my harm?*

Paul asks a difficult question regarding our response to God's gracious movement toward us: "Or do you show contempt for the riches of his kindness, forbearance and patience, not realizing that God's kindness is intended to lead you to repentance?" (Romans 2:4). When someone gives us a gift, we stiffen when we doubt their sincerity, fear that our desire for more will increase beyond our control, or recoil in the sense that our sinfulness makes us unlovable. Contempt is a defense against the naked shame that comes when love penetrates a sinful heart.

Ungodly contempt dulls the ups and downs of ambivalence and aggressively demands distance; since God's love does not seem clear, I am justified to act on my own behalf. Contempt vocalizes the core question, *Does God love me, or will He turn away in disgust?*

Shame: A Flight from Intimacy

Shame is a flight from intimacy. It is one of our deepest fears: We will be isolated and mocked forever. It is a taste of hell—the experience of being caught without defense or cover and condemned to unrelenting humiliation.

Shame is feeling exposed as ugly beyond words. Nothing else cuts to the core so personally as shame does. Philosopher Jean-Paul Sartre referred to it as a "hemorrhage of the soul."

Shame drains us of energy and withers our desire to exist. Like other emotions of flight (fear and despair), shame is a withdrawal from engagement. Its typical posture is eyes downcast, shoulders slumped, heart disengaged. Shame is an escape from reality through dissociation.

Ungodly shame dulls the terror of exposure and passively demands safety; since God's love seems dangerous, I am justified in shutting down. Shame vocalizes the core question, *Does God love me, or will He hate me if He sees me as I really am?*

Most of us seek to escape from shame by spending our energy insulating ourselves from anything or anyone that might provoke exposure.

A woman who refuses to learn to ski explained, "I haven't learned a new sport since I was a kid. It's not that I'm afraid of falling or hurting myself. I remember how I hated trying something new with others around who knew how to do it. They looked at me with such disgust, I swore I would never humiliate myself learning something new again."

Others choose spouses or careers on the same basis. "Will this person or activity expose me to humiliation, shame, mockery? If so, then I refuse to move into that arena." Many refuse to speak about their inner convictions or faith because they fear being mocked.

Shame seems to justify avoidance. Even more, it seems to demand the insulation of arrogance. This is shamelessness—immunity to shame through progressive hardening of the heart.

Arrogance is more than a cocky attitude or boasting about personal competence; it is a clenched fist shaken at the heavens in defiance: "I will not bow; I will not be broken by the weight of reality. I will not succumb to the desire for reconciliation. I will not face, nor feel, the groaning of my soul for redemption." Arrogance can show itself in contemptuous belligerence or in the quiet refusal, or supposed inability, to feel. Arrogance involves turning away from the groaning of our soul—and, therefore, turning away from struggling with God.

What does the struggle with God look like? What is the battle that we must fight with God if we are to know Him with depth and passion?

The answer is that each of us must wrestle with the complaint, "How long, O Lord?" Each of our difficult emotions—anger, fear, jealousy, despair, contempt, and shame—opens the door for that question to be exposed and answered through the mystery of God's involvement with us.

4

—

Unrighteous Anger: A Refusal to Wait for Justice

Anger can well up suddenly like a geyser, spewing out scalding water on all who stand too close. Or it can smolder and burn under the surface for interminable periods, burning all that stands in its path.

Anger is our response to an assault. Its intensity is usually in accord with the degree of perceived injustice, though the assault need not be real or severe to draw forth an extreme response. Further, if the assault blocks earnest desire, or what we believe we must possess in order to be whole, then we will burn with rage.

WHAT PROVOKES ANGER?

Interference with Satisfaction

Imagine being stuck in a traffic jam. You check your watch and wonder if the traffic will unsnarl soon. You have ten minutes to make an important appointment; if you could get to the next exit just two hundred yards down the highway, you could easily be there on time. You blame yourself for not leaving earlier. You curse your bad luck, the highway department, and the lousy driver who likely rear-ended another car. The anger directed toward yourself and others does not take away the desire to be on time, but it allows you, at least momentarily, to escape the panic of waiting and the pain of hoping the traffic will clear.

To be blocked from gaining what we want forces us to wait, and we despise the helplessness of waiting because it stops us from moving toward satisfaction. We are distressed when we are compelled to wait in a bank line or for a friend who is late. The break in momentum toward satisfaction tells us that relief is not imminent; in fact, it might not occur at all. Waiting intensifies pain because it forces us to see that we are dependent creatures.

Unjust Assault

We want satisfaction—the resolution of our tension and emptiness—but we can't obtain relief because satisfaction of our deepest desire is in the hands of those we can't control. We feel irritated when others do not comply with our desires, but our anger seems utterly justified when our desires are not satisfied because of injustice.

Let's say that you're heading for a drinking fountain when someone steps in front of you. You're momentarily frustrated because you want to satisfy your thirst and someone has blocked your desire.

If you get your turn at the fountain soon enough, your frustration will disappear. But if the person in front of you drinks too slowly and threatens your imminent satisfaction, you will likely feel irritation. Waiting intensifies your discomfort. But if the dawdling drinker then calls a child over to get a drink, your irritation may shift into anger. "Why doesn't she make the child wait in line? I waited in line—it's not fair!"

Every true assault involves some form of injustice. An injustice is any violation of God's design for life. We ought to feel irritated when a thoughtless person litters trash, violating the beauty of creation. But this is usually a relatively minor injustice. The person who pulls the trigger of a gun and leaves an innocent child paralyzed commits a devastating injustice. The greater the injustice, the more anger we ought to feel. To read about a child paralyzed by a gang shooting and not feel anger is unholy.

Listen to the voice of one man who was full of anger about unjust assault:

> My God, whom I praise,
>   do not remain silent,
> for people who are wicked and deceitful
>   have opened their mouths against me;
>   they have spoken against me with lying tongues.
> With words of hatred they surround me;
>   they attack me without cause. . . .
> Appoint someone evil to oppose my enemy;
>   let an accuser stand at his right hand.
> When he is tried, let him be found guilty,
>   and may his prayers condemn him.
> May his days be few;
>   may another take his place of leadership.
> May his children be fatherless
>   and his wife a widow.
> May his children be wandering beggars;
>   may they be driven from their ruined homes.
> *Psalm 109:1-3, 6-10*

David was angry. He wanted vengeance—payment that extended to the entire family of the man who harmed him. Imprecatory psalms are full of fury. The psalmist desires to see harm return to those whose assault has brought him agony. Is it biblical? Can an angry heart that prays for harm also be a good heart? C. S. Lewis believed these psalms did not reflect Christian virtue, but rather the Old Testament ethic of an eye for an eye. What is the place of anger in Christian life?

God designed and blessed anger in order to energize our passion to destroy sin. Anger can be lovely and redemptive, but it can also be ugly and vindictive. It depends in part on the object of the anger, how it is expressed, and why the anger is unleashed.

The anger expressed in most interactions has little to do with the redemptive purpose of destroying ugliness in order to enhance what is good. The person filled with unrighteous anger suppresses the freedom of others, trying to force submission. His anger consumes the other, filling an emptiness that demands satisfaction and refuses to cry out in humble, vulnerable need. Unrighteous anger condemns any who stand opposed to its pursuit of control. As James says, "Human anger does not produce the righteousness that God desires" (James 1:20).

Are we to assume that all anger is simply wrong? Paul tells us, "In your anger do not sin" (Ephesians 4:26). He presumes that not all anger is sin, and that we can be angry without being dominated by sin. How is this accomplished? The answer lies in the distinction between unrighteous and righteous anger. In this chapter we will explore unrighteous anger; in the next chapter we will explore righteous anger as a reflection of God's character.

UNRIGHTEOUS ANGER:
A DEMAND FOR JUSTICE NOW

Unrighteous anger is a dark energy that demands for the self a more tolerable world *now*, instead of waiting for God's redemption according to divine design and timing.

Unrighteous Anger Suppresses Choice

Quentin was washing carrots in the sink before peeling them. His sister-in-law, Sarah, was visiting at the time. As she came into the kitchen, he heard her voice rise an octave and in volume. The sound was like the rattle of a poisonous snake. Sarah was coiled and ready for assault, and it would only be a matter of moments before someone was going to feel her bite.

Children scurried away faster than acceptable by polite standards. They knew enough to flee, but they hadn't yet developed the sophistication to move as if they were going somewhere else. A few other adults in the kitchen also departed stage left, but years of practice gave their flight a refinement that hid their childlike terror.

Quentin, caught in the middle of his culinary task, could not escape. Sarah finally bit. "Really, now, what is wrong with you!" she scolded him, her voice laced with sarcasm. "Don't you know you don't have to wash carrots if you're going to peel them?"

Quentin refrained from looking her in the face. "Yeah, well," he mumbled, "I'll just finish what I started." He finished peeling the carrots and then, as soon as he could, left the kitchen for safer ground.

Who knew what provoked Sarah's attack? It wasn't the most severe, but its rancid odor lingered in the air and set the tone for the rest of the evening. Perhaps that was her point. Sarah's anger was a trident that enforced her divine prerogatives, intimidating others. They were no longer free to make their own choices—choices that might have left Sarah feeling shamed, empty, lonely, or vulnerable to attack.

Righteous anger, on the other hand, does not suppress choice. Instead, it unnerves by offering a taste of pain in order to compel change.

Unrighteous Anger Consumes Others

Another aim of unrighteous anger is to acquire whatever will fill emptiness and then defend the fragile hold on that claim. This is the spirit of possession.

My (Dan's) five-year-old son was recently given a new tractor by a neighbor. One day when Andrew was not playing with it, his sister decided to try out the toy. From across the street came a howl of indignation as Andrew screamed, "Amanda! Get off my new toy. It's mine, mine, mine!" His little body shook with rage as he descended on her with a flurry of blows.

Unrighteous anger attempts to control the choices of others, especially in regard to our attempt to possess what we believe is essential to our well-being.

My son's attack against his sister was invigorated by his repetitious call to arms: "It's mine, mine, mine!" He believed with his heart and soul that he "owned" the tractor, that he "needed" the toy, and that he would "perish" if someone else touched it.

We are committed to the idolatrous demand of experiencing the fullness of heaven *now*. Our anger is designed to possess whatever taste of heaven we can find now and preserve that small sliver of satisfaction.

To possess others means to devour them to fill our emptiness. Hunger seems to justify our efforts to consume and violate. The Psalms compare this behavior to dogs who prowl for something to devour and howl when they are empty: "They return at evening, snarling like dogs, and prowl about the city. They wander about for food and howl if not satisfied" (59:14-15). A pack of dogs will attack and kill any prey that might fill their emptiness. They are not concerned about when or what they eat—only that their stomachs are full.

A client confessed that she spent hours every day plotting how to keep her husband involved with her. She concocted varying sexual scenes; she planned sports outings, vacations, and relaxing nights in front of the television. Everything was done with compulsive intensity. The emotion sustaining her frenetic "service" was not love, respect, or tenderness; it was rage. Her husband was her "meal," and she prowled and howled until her stomach was full.

Isaiah points to a relationship between frenetic activity and rage.

The poetic form of the verse underlines the strong relationship between emptiness, frantic searching, and rage: "Distressed and hungry, they will roam through the land; when they are famished, they will become enraged" (Isaiah 8:21).

Solomon makes the same point regarding human striving, commenting on all efforts to succeed, "I saw that all toil and all achievement spring from one person's envy of another. This too is meaningless, a chasing after the wind" (Ecclesiastes 4:4). Our frantic chasing after achievement might not feel like envy or anger, but that is its fuel.

When the topic of anger came up in counseling with the frenetic wife, she was baffled. She was aware only of pressure and fear. She *had* to please her husband, because she was scared he would leave her.

Eventually, however, she owned up to a steel-like hardness— an angry flash that occasionally showed itself when her plans for a romantic evening were frustrated. In those instances, her anger drew blood by undermining her husband's virility, job performance, and effectiveness as a father. Her comments were well-placed stabs that left him defensive and weak.

Anger was what sustained this woman's drive to gain love. It showed itself when she felt defeated by circumstances. And it drew her back into the battle, restoring her hope that she might clutch victory. Her anger energized her pursuit to gain satisfaction and punish her husband when he seemed to fail her.

Unrighteous anger condemns any who stand in its way; righteous anger desires to bless—to fill life rather than drain it.

Unrighteous Anger Condemns Others

Anger suppresses choice. It fuels our frantic efforts to seize fullness. But it goes beyond control and possession to annihilation. Unrighteous anger always harbors the hatred of Cain—it kills to make someone pay for exposure and pain.

A teenage boy recently died in a shooting because he had looked another driver in the eye at a traffic light. His killer said: "He dissed me. He had to die." Unrighteous anger wants to destroy.

The anger inside us wants to rampage, to dethrone authority, to violate. In the midst of roaming and raging, the fallen heart curses. A curse is the release of rage. Ineffective as it is to shout, scream, and curse, it is a means of reclaiming the illusion of power in the face of feeling impotent. I may be defeated, but I can boast in the final hurrah of arrogance—"bent and bloody, but not broken," as one poet put it.

Although our anger may be directed against others, ultimately we are directing our curses against God. Even when our anger is directed against inanimate objects, it is an attack against the Creator. We are furious at God for inequality. He has made some more lovely, intelligent, and gifted than others. He does not dispense opportunity and talent equally. God also seems to be either unable or unwilling to address injustice; sometimes it even feels as if He is on the side of evil, joining the assault against us. We want vengeance.

The desire to violate is our repayment to God and others for the emptiness and harm that is not recompensed. It is an attack against an attack. And it will not be satisfied until the other is defeated, humiliated, and utterly annihilated.

Contrast unrighteous to righteous anger—righteous anger wounds when the warning and the desire to bless continue to be violated. Anger is a taste of hell that calls the arrogant offender to repentance. It is a weapon that exposes, invites change, and provokes pain—all for the sake of compelling the one who did harm to deal with their sin.

UNRIGHTEOUS ANGER IS A BATTLE AGAINST GOD

If the essence of righteous anger is a hatred of sin and a love of beauty, then the core of unrighteous anger is a hatred of vulnerability and a love of control. Unrighteous anger seeks to gain independence from God and others. Psalm 2 describes the motivation of foolish anger:

> Why do the nations conspire
>   and the peoples plot in vain?
> The kings of the earth rise up
>   and the rulers band together
>   against the LORD and against his anointed, saying,
> "Let us break their chains
>   and throw off their shackles."
> *Psalm 2:1-3*

Why do the people of this world rage? It is because they want to be free of their chains and shackles. They want to cut loose and do as they desire. They do not want the restraint placed on them by the rule of God. Unrighteous anger is a hammer that tries to break the bond of servitude connecting us to our Creator.

Unrighteous anger delivers us from trusting a God who does not comply with our desires. Oddly, however, unrighteous anger also draws our deepest desires to the surface and leaves us even emptier than we were before. It is the exposure of unrighteous anger's impotency that leaves us naked before the expected anger of God.

But what we encounter when we rage against God and others is not what we expect. We expect judgment, anticipating that His rage will be turned inexhaustibly upon us. Instead, His glorious, perfect Son bears the wrath we deserve. What are we to learn about anger from God's odd wrath?

5

—

Righteous Anger:
An Assault against Injustice

The assault was not severe. My words might have been considered an innocent, off-the-cuff remark, but they were laced with a dash of sarcasm.

I (Dan) had made a mistake that was going to cost me some extra money and time. I told Susan, my personal assistant, "Well, if you take less time for lunch breaks, maybe we can make up the loss over a year." It was quickly said and, on my part, as rapidly forgotten.

Several days later, Susan asked for some time. We sat down and she said, "Do you have any concerns about my work?"

"Absolutely not," I replied. "Why?"

"Tuesday," she explained, "you made a remark about my lunch-time and I wondered if you had any concerns or if your comment was something that came out of your frustration."

Suddenly, I felt embarrassed. I recalled the remark and wished Susan would go away. I assured her I had no concerns and I was thrilled about her work and her heart for the ministry and me. I hoped my "compliment" would end the discussion and bury my small-minded remark under my gift offering.

But she was angry. She did not take my gift and waltz out of the room. Instead, she leaned forward in her chair and said, "Sometimes, I cannot tell when your teasing is fun and when it hides meanness." Her voice was tender and strong. Her eyes were full of pain and anger.

I allowed her remark to roll off my back, and I agreed it must be difficult. But then she spoke with even greater intensity: "I don't know what it would be like for you to so deeply desire to be like the Lord and also so easily hurt others."

I was taken back by the intensity of her words and the kindness in her eyes. I wanted to run, hide, weep, lash out, but instead I felt exposed and invited to reflect on God's involvement with me. Susan's anger was righteous and redemptive. In this world, it is also rare.

Righteous anger warns, invites, and wounds for the greater work of redemption. It is full of a strength that is neither defensive nor vindictive, and it is permeated by a sadness that is rich in desire and hope. Most importantly, righteous anger allows the offense to be seen as an issue between the offender and God.

How does righteous anger arise in hearts that are so well acquainted with controlling, possessive, condemning anger?

RIGHTEOUS ANGER IS WILLING TO STRUGGLE AND WAIT

Our initial reaction of anger to any perceived injustice may be righteous or unrighteous—it is nearly impossible to evaluate. Only the absence of anger is noteworthy as an indication that something is terribly wrong.

What happens *after* the initial arousal of anger, however, can be assessed. Righteous anger grieves and struggles with God: "What are

You doing, God? What am I to understand about You? What am I to face about myself, given the fury I feel?"

Listen to the force of angry confusion in the voice of the psalmist:

My heart meditated and my spirit asked:
"Will the Lord reject forever?
Will he never show his favor again?
Has his unfailing love vanished forever?
Has his promise failed for all time?
Has God forgotten to be merciful?
Has he in anger withheld his compassion?"

Psalm 77:6-9

But his focus moves from his hurt and anger toward God to pondering the character and deeds of God (verses 10-11). Our reaction to the pain and injustice of life will only move toward godly anger if we own up to our struggle with God and move toward Him with our questions.

Unrighteous anger refuses to turn to God with our deepest questions—"Are You just? Are You going to let the wicked win? Are You going to let them violate me with no justice in sight?" In the midst of helpless confusion and hurt, unrighteous anger refuses to surrender, to wait on God, to look to Him for perspective. Instead, we feel righteous in taking justice into our hands when the One we cry to for justice does not hear or respond. We become vigilantes, seeking to impose our own sense of justice according to the demands of our desire.

The apostle James describes our fury over frustrated desire in these terms:

You desire but do not have, so you kill. You covet but you cannot get what you want, so you quarrel and fight. You do

not have because you do not ask God. When you ask, you
do not receive, because you ask with wrong motives, that
you may spend what you get on your pleasures.

James 4:2-3

When our desires go unsatisfied, we become murderous. It is inevitable unless we deal with the idolatry of desire and surrender to God. But that is the rub. He is the one who could satisfy our emptiness; and He does not do as we demand. He makes us wait, and the wait intensifies our desire and exposes our loss of control—compelling us either to trust Him or to turn against Him.

Unrighteous anger trusts in its own power and might, refusing to hope in God. It's no surprise that the Bible links hope in God with a willingness to wait:

Wait for the LORD;
  be strong and take heart
  and wait for the LORD.

Psalm 27:14

We wait in hope for the LORD;
  he is our help and our shield.

Psalm 33:20

I wait for the LORD, my whole being waits,
  and in his word I put my hope.

Psalm 130:5

To wait is to have confidence that God will bring justice. He will satisfy the depths of our desire, but it will happen in His time and not ours. The heart that offers righteous anger continues to struggle with confusion—*God, what are You doing?* But the confusion directs the heart toward God, rather than triggering a flight from doubt through dogmatism or hardening the hurt through rebellion. In the struggle with God, the righteous heart waits for God to reveal His character.

THE SURPRISING GLORY OF ANGER

Our dark emotions are stained emblems of the sure, solid image of God. Our ugliest, most destructive emotions reflect something of the glory of God; consequently, they reflect, however poorly and darkly, the glory and honor of our humanity. They're like a photographic negative. A negative is an inversion of what really exists. Everything that is black is a reflection of what will be light.

To understand God's character, we must look at what our dark emotions reveal about His glory. How do our unrighteous irritation, frustration, anger, rage, and fury reflect the glory of God?

The fury to shame and annihilate reflects the righteous rage God intends for us to feel in order to mock the evil one and destroy sin. The anger that possesses another in order to fill emptiness points to the jealousy to protect others that God intends for us to feel. The dark side bears the imprint of what God intended.

How is dark rage an inverted picture of His bright, lovely intention for anger?

Oddly, even our unrighteous desire to destroy still reflects a legitimate, God-honoring fury. The Psalms are full of imprecatory fury. An imprecatory psalm is a bloody plea for God to destroy an enemy, a howl of indignation demanding that evil suffer:

> By your hand save me from such people, Lord,
>   from those of this world whose reward is in this life.
> *Psalm 17:14*

But do not kill them, Lord our shield,
    or my people will forget.
In your might uproot them
    and bring them down.
Psalm 59:11

May they be blotted out of the book of life
    and not be listed with the righteous.
Psalm 69:28

May his children be fatherless
    and his wife a widow.
May his children be wandering beggars;
    may they be driven from their ruined homes.
May a creditor seize all he has;
    may strangers plunder the fruits of his labor.
May no one extend kindness to him
    or take pity on his fatherless children.
Psalm 109:9-12

Happy is the one who seizes your infants
    and dashes them against the rocks.
Psalm 137:9

It is not enough merely to see the enemy killed. The psalmist wants him staggered, shamed, wiped out of the book of life. And not only should he suffer, but his children and wife ought to bear the onus of his crimes. It is even preferable to see his children's heads smashed against a rock.

Christians are never angry enough. We have learned to distance ourselves from anger, irrespective of whether it is righteous or unrighteous. And when is righteous anger not stained by unrighteous motivation? Never. Equally, unrighteous anger will always reflect a hint of what and how we are to hate. If our anger must wait for perfect purity to be honored and expressed, then we are better off as frozen, unfeeling automatons.

Our human anger may sometimes need to be silenced, but other times it may need to be spoken. Our hope must be that our anger will grow more righteous as we are shaped to the contours of God's anger. If we allow ourselves to join God's fury and then focus on what we are to hate—evil, sin, ugliness—our hearts may discover a new dimension of the character of God.

THE SURPRISING ANGER OF GOD

God's anger is paradoxical. On one hand, He is "gracious and compassionate, slow to anger and rich in love" (Psalm 145:8). On the other, He is the one who "unleashed against them his hot anger, his wrath, indignation and hostility—a band of destroying angels" (Psalm 78:49). Psalm 78 even compares Him to a drunk who awakens with a hangover and unleashes his hot fury against his enemies: "Then the Lord awoke as from sleep, as a warrior wakes from the stupor of wine. He beat back his enemies; he put them to everlasting shame" (verses 65-66).

Which is God—slow and reasoned, or hot and impulsive? The paradox is that He is both. The message seems to be simple: It takes a lot to provoke God's rage, but when it comes, it is hot, hard, and consuming. It's best not to test His anger.

But God's anger comes for a holy purpose: to provoke fear ("leave your sin or be destroyed") and dismantle those who do not heed His warning. The psalmist links God's anger and our fear:

We are consumed by your anger
    and terrified by your indignation.

You have set our iniquities before you,
    our secret sins in the light of your presence.
All our days pass away under your wrath;
    we finish our years with a moan.
Our days may come to seventy years;
    or eighty, if our strength endures;
yet the best of them are but trouble and sorrow,
    for they quickly pass, and we fly away.
If only we knew the power of your anger!
    Your wrath is as great as the fear that is your due.
Teach us to number our days,
    that we may gain a heart of wisdom.
Psalm 90:7-12

God's wrath is commensurate with the fear that is due Him. If we refuse to bow to Him, we will face His anger, dismantling the presumption of our independence. The psalmist declares that under the weight of God's anger, his health vanishes (38:1-3); he is unable to move (88:7-8); he staggers like a man forced to drink the cup of God's wrath (60:1-3). God's anger tears down our self-sufficiency and compels us to take Him into account.

God's anger warns, invites change, and finally punishes. Anger is the weapon of dominion. It is a voice of strength that challenges chaos, destroys sin, and redeems ugliness.

What is most inconceivable, however, is that the focus of God's rage against sin has not been directed against us, but against Himself. He promised to make the arrogant drink a foaming cup of His wrath, a reflection of God's furious hatred of sin. The arrogant would then stagger and die. But the one who drank this bitter, foaming cup of wrath was Jesus. It is beyond our comprehension—the perfect Adam, loved and adored by the Father, was also despised by the Father. God the Father turned against His Son, and for a moment the unity of the Trinity was splintered under the weight of the wrath of God.

Consequently, we are promised that we will never bear the weight of His staggering fury. It has already been poured out on the perfect human being—the glorious Son.

THE TRANSFORMATION OF UNRIGHTEOUS ANGER

Our desire to destroy may one day reflect God's hatred of anything that mars His glory and His creation. He invites us to marvel at the One who receives His rage and rejoice that it is not us. Further, He invites us to pour out our anger before Him, so that our anger might eventually be turned against the one who most deserves it—the evil one.

What are we to do with our anger now? Are we simply to call our unrighteous anger wrong, turn from it, and choose to be kind? We are certainly to do no less, but we are to invited to do much more: We are called to ponder and marvel.

The psalmist tells us that when we are angry, we should be still and ponder. We are not asked simply to eliminate a destructive feeling and replace it with a constructive one. But we are asked to be willing to wait and reflect.

Be Still

"Be still before the LORD and wait patiently for him; do not fret when people succeed in their ways, when they carry out their wicked schemes. Refrain from anger and turn from wrath; do not fret—it leads only to evil" (Psalm 37:7-8).

When you are angry, wait. Stop, sit, don't move! Anger is a catalyst that stirs us into battle. Most of the battles that anger will draw us into fighting are not worthy of our blood. Unrighteous anger will never deepen our heart for God or others unless we are willing to go through anger detox.

Detoxification of anger is writhing with the desire to strike out and choosing not to release the anger—either toward another person or toward an inanimate object. Be still. Sit with your rage, let it rack you like a buffeting wind and a harsh rain. Let its fury soak you in the sweat of desire.

Wait

Waiting does not deny, nor does it pretend. It is not merely taking a time-out. It is entering the very soil that drew the rage to the surface—the fury against God for requiring us to wait to see His justice and goodness. Choosing to be still opens the heart to even deeper dimensions of anger that go beyond the situation to the God who seems so silent, withdrawn, or against us.

Obviously, being still avoids the initial damage and repercussions of wickedly chosen anger, but its true purpose is to drive us into a deeper battle with God.

Ponder

"In your anger do not sin; when you are on your beds, search your hearts and be silent" (Psalm 4:4).

Anger should lead us into silent pondering rather than direct action. Usually, anger is a starting gun that signals us to leap from the blocks to control, consume, destroy. Instead, anger should be a starting gun that calls us to sit down and think.

What are we to ponder?

Ponder your desire. What do you really want to do? You have been gripped by a strong passion to control, consume, and destroy—but does it reflect the depths of your redeemed passion? Instead, is there not a deeper desire to warn, invite change, and punish sin in order to destroy the ugly cancer growing in the person who has brought pain to your heart? If not, ponder what is the hardness that has clogged your heart's redemptive desire.

Ponder your sin. Jesus advised that we consider the log in our own eye before we deal with the speck in another's eye. Whatever failure or assault we hate in others, we must hate in ourselves as well. If we hate their sin more than our own, we will always be unrighteous. But if we hate the sin in our own hearts more than what we see in theirs, we will grow in the quiet, patient sorrow of true righteous anger.

Ponder God. Whatever your fury, it is only a speck of what God felt and delivered against His Son for your sake. If your rage compels you to smash your fist on a table, consider the blow as a reminder of what the Father already carried out against the Son. What kind of God is He, to turn His fist-smashing wrath against Himself rather than against you? Awe of God must grow if our anger is to deepen in the direction of righteousness.

Pondering the character of God does not pacify anger; it deepens it. Our struggle is never that we are too angry, but that we are never angry enough. Our anger is always pitifully small when it is focused against a person or object; it is meant to be turned against all evil and all sin—beginning first with our own failure of love. In order to deepen righteous anger we must learn what it is to join the anger of God.

LIVING OUT OF RIGHTEOUS ANGER

What does righteous anger look like? What does it hope to accomplish?

Righteous anger warns, invites change, and wounds. True anger is paradoxical in that it has the strength to inflict pain, but it burns with the desire for reconciliation. It is bold, but it is also broken.

Righteous anger exposes. It is a warning to the unwary: *Danger ahead!* It is a call that says, *Watch out! You are in danger of violating love, of doing damage to yourself and others.* The warning informs the offender that a violation or assault has occurred. It exposes failure and draws attention to the cancer that might destroy the heart.

It is never our right to take away freedom and responsibility of choice. It is our privilege to draw attention to the potential harm and leave the decision to the other. Those who indulge in unrighteous anger refuse to bear the pain and grief of what others may do with their freedom. Instead, they suppress freedom in order to ensure that they will not be left empty. Righteous anger never suppresses choice—it merely exposes the potential for ill.

When Susan came to me to ask about my concerns regarding her work, she was exposing my harm. An exposure is not a defensive, hands-on-the-hips retort that returns one attack for another. It is rather a bold, eye-to-eye engagement that makes it clear that the original attack is not going to work to gain illegitimate power.

My comment about Susan's lunch breaks in effect punished her for my financial failure. Her question exposed my frail assault and forced me to acknowledge I had no basis of concern about her work. She stood up to my assault and exposed my sin.

Righteous anger invites change. It can envision what the other might look like if the arrogance controlling the heart was pierced. Anger is a surgical weapon, designed to destroy ugliness and restore beauty. In the hands of one who is trained in love and who can envision beauty, the knife of righteous anger is a weapon for restoration.

We can wield the weapon of righteous anger only if we believe in the wonder of redemption—not a belief *about* redemption, nor an intellectual assent *to* redemption, but a belief born of God's pursuit that has personally turned our hearts topsy-turvy in joy, sorrow, confusion, and wonder. True, our hearts may also battle with bitterness, but they will hold a strange warmth that equally longs to bless the offender.

The desire to bless, to see redemption, will be experienced, in part, as the labor pains of birth. Susan's pain on my behalf and her hope to see me struggle with my failure was more disturbing than the exposure of my offense. Her tears tenderized her anger and made it nearly impossible to dismiss her.

It is a costly gift to be redemptively angry at one who offended you. It is far easier to feel no anger. But the absence of anger is the choice to remain unaffected by sin. Righteous anger is called for when we see God's glory violated.

This is a tall order, to say the least. It is easier to mask our anger through busyness or even deny the anger by blaming ourselves. It is safer merely to be irked on the surface and then go away and privately fantasize harm. Righteous anger moves beyond the private domain of fantasy into the realm of inviting the offender to struggle with the damage done and walk the path of restoration.

Righteous anger must do more than invite the offender to change; it must invite him to marvel at where God focuses His staggering fury. This can be done only if our anger is interlaced with sorrow—sadness for one's own loss, a grief for the loss of the offender, and most of all, a sorrow for the pain God feels as He sees His creation war against itself. Our pain is to be a bridge to comprehending the pain of God. He grieves for both victim and abuser. He feels sadness for the pain of His children and the arrogance involved in all sin.

Righteous anger wounds. Righteous indignation can be intense; it is never a mere explosion of fury. It is focused and direct; it is never a spewing out of accusations and invective. It wounds in order to heal. Fredrick Buechner has described a friend as one who gives and receives wounds. Righteous anger is a blow that hopes to inoculate the other from the potential of even greater harm. In that sense, righteous anger is like punishing our children. It serves the purpose of inflicting pain in order to escape the horror of even more destructive harm.

Our destructive anger will be transformed into righteous anger as we grow in hatred of evil and love of good. To be righteously angry, we must be consumed by a holy fear of God.

6

—

Unrighteous Fear:
A Destructive Anxiety

Sweeping the kitchen floor, Theresa thought about the day's activities. Life was so busy that it was only at moments like these that she could indulge in daydreaming and planning. Even so, she had to hurry in order to make it to the women's Bible study at church. After that, she had scheduled a planning lunch with her garden club, which could last a couple of hours.

Suddenly she noticed a quiet growling from within, a slight gnawing in her stomach. Her vacant thoughts were filled with the picture of her teenage son, Robert. He had sullenly walked out of the house that morning, mumbling as he left: "Life stinks."

She stopped sweeping. She felt out of breath, even dizzy. She collected herself and began sweeping again but found it hard to focus on her work. Then she realized that she had been standing still for some minutes, simply staring into space. A rash of pictures flooded her mind about Robert; fear gripped and plunged her into torment.

He had no friends; he seemed so lonely. At home, he moped

around the house and lacked the motivation to do his homework. The homeroom teacher had called yesterday expressing her concern about his work and attitude. The picture of him doing harm to himself hovered before her like a demon.

Her mouth was dry, so she went to get a drink of water. She started to sit down, but felt herself on the edge of tears. Catching herself, she forced herself up, finished sweeping the floor, and pushed the thoughts out of her mind.

FEAR: UNCERTAINTY IN THE FACE OF DANGER

Fear isn't only the terror we feel at the announcement of life-threatening news. It isn't only a reaction to the threat of physical pain or harm. It is also the everyday uncertainty that gnaws at us. The slightest things may trigger it.

Some of the forms that fear takes are worry, nervousness, and angst. Sometimes it's free-floating, apparently without a specific cause—everything worries us. At other times, we know all too well what triggers it: an imposing boss, a neglectful or irresponsible spouse, a troubled teen, even a messy desk.

We could list an entire spectrum of feelings under the heading "fear," in ascending order of intensity: nervousness . . . worry . . . anxiety . . . terror . . . horror. The difference between them has to do with the intensity of the feeling, not necessarily the seriousness of the problem that evokes the fear. The two do not always match.

One woman feels very anxious if her kitchen floor is dirty. Others survive quite well with an entire house in disarray. Some of my (Tremper's) students can't sleep the night before an exam. They worry that I'll ask a question they can't answer. Other students don't even give it a second thought. They study as much as they can and then sleep deeply. Interestingly, the grades don't reflect the amount of worry they put into it!

Worry and fear are first cousins. They vary in intensity but are both forms of the same emotion. What causes them?

Different people fear different things with different levels of intensity, but *all of us fear what we cannot control*. Fear is our response to uncertainty about our resources in the face of danger, when we are assaulted by a force that overwhelms us and compels us to face that we are helpless and out of control. Fear is provoked when the threat of danger (physical or relational) exposes our inability to preserve what we most deeply cherish.

Theresa could not do anything to help her son Robert. He was independent of her guidance and control. If he refused to face his hurt, she could pray, talk, and solicit the help of others, but she could not compel him to change. If he chose to slip deeper into depression, she could seek professional help, but ultimately, she could not keep him from taking his life.

All fear involves the threat of danger. The Bible tells us that we live in a fallen world filled with sinful human beings. Satan, the embodiment of evil, is called "the prince of this world." Christians know that the world is full of threat and danger. Every day can bring trouble, whether difficulties at work with associates or broken relationships in the home. Perhaps the greatest threats are those we cannot control.

SEPARATION AND DEATH: THE ULTIMATE THREAT

It was thirty years ago, when I (Tremper) was about ten years old, but the memory is as vivid as if it happened yesterday. I was looking out the window of my bedroom when it suddenly hit me that I was going to die. Sure, I knew that flowers, animals, and even people died. But I had never before faced the reality of *my* death, and I was horrified.

For the next year as I drifted off to sleep each night, I would imagine a tombstone with my name on it. I didn't think I would die at that moment, or even relatively soon, but I knew that death was inevitable. There was no escape.

Now that I'm older, death is a reality that I have witnessed. And to be honest, it is no less horrible a thought to me now than when I was ten years old. Indeed, equally frightening is the experience of growing old, losing physical and mental abilities, ending up like some of my older relatives in a nursing home, helpless to get up from the bed by myself, unable to speak a coherent word.

Death, pain, and suffering are dangers that lurk behind every corner and under every bed. Most of us realize at an early age that danger exists, and that it can destroy us. And we know that we are impotent against the inevitability of death.

The book of Ecclesiastes drives home the significance of the horror of death. The teacher fully realizes that death not only brings life to a tragic conclusion, it renders meaningless every earthly status and achievement.

We fear physical and personal death. We fear dissolution, fragmentation, coming apart at the seams, non-being. We feel fear whenever death—the dissolution of order and coherence—plunges us into the dark unknown.

The psalmist, too, feared death. He did not try to hide his fear from God. Especially when he was sick (and there are a number of psalms sung by the psalmist when he was sick), he cried out in terror to the Lord to save him from the grave. Psalm 30 is actually a thanksgiving psalm, giving praise to God for saving the psalmist from death, but in the process of celebrating his healing, the psalmist quotes his earlier lament to God:

What is gained if I am silenced,
    if I go down to the pit?
Will the dust praise you?
    Will it proclaim your faithfulness?

Hear, LORD, and be merciful to me;
  LORD, be my help.
Psalm 30:9-10

At the heart of the fear of death is the terror of separation. Death is the ultimate experience of loneliness. When we die, those things and people who give us joy are gone forever. Indeed, when seen apart from the gospel, death separates us even from ourselves.

Death is a physical reality, but it is also symbolic. We feel fear when core, life-giving dreams that are the basis of our personal identity are threatened with extinction. I (Tremper) remember the tortuous months of waiting to hear from graduate schools. I had finished college with excellent grades and was in my last year of seminary, graduating at the top of my class academically. My teachers were all urging me to go to an outstanding graduate school.

But after spending hours filling out all the application forms, getting references and transcripts sent in, and mailing them all to six graduate schools, I felt an acute terror. After about one week, I approached the mailbox with absolute fear, hands trembling as I uttered ritual prayers beseeching God that I be greeted by acceptance letters.

Of course it took six months for me to hear from the schools, but each day at mail time, my body shook and my mind froze. The death of the dream of graduate school felt like the potential death of my identity. Any form of death has the potential to evoke great fear.

The reality of death drives home the fact that everyone experiences fear. Even if your life is perfect, every relationship a success, and every aspect of your life in order, you have something to fear—the dark, unknown reality of death. Indeed, I would argue that those who are most happy in this life are also the most fearful of death. Death means separation from the status you get from your work, the respect you receive from others, the benefits of your material possessions, the presence of your loved ones.

HELPLESSNESS AND FLIGHT

Danger also exposes our impotence to preserve what matters most to us: our happiness. The more important the concern, the more helpless we are to preserve it. I can keep my yard green and virtually free from weeds. But I cannot ensure that my children will grow in the Lord and be free from the entanglements of sin.

Daily life tends to shield us from our real helplessness to the extent that it preserves our illusion of power and control. We can plan a trip or finish a project, and we feel powerful. But the effect of our labor can be undone in an instant, and we are helpless to keep that dissolution at bay.

Dreams often expose our basic fear by giving us vivid glimpses of it. Most of the time I (Dan) find it hard to recall a dream even moments after I wake, but this one is a classic I have repeated over the years.

The dream begins as I walk into an Algebra I class, not having attended for ten weeks, to discover that we are taking the final exam. A long series of algebraic hieroglyphics are scribbled over the page, and I must give the answer and show how I arrived at my conclusion. I start to write with fury. At first, the movement of my pen feels wonderful. I have no idea what I'm doing, but the work is progressing.

Out of the corner of my eye, I see the teacher walking toward my desk. I huddle over my paper and continue to produce page after page of symbols. His movement toward me grows faster and faster and I, in turn, write more quickly until everything feels like a blur.

All of a sudden I am in front of the entire class, and my pages and pages of response are spilling out of my hands. The teacher picks up a page, and I can feel myself grow small and pale. The teacher's face turns cruel, and contemptuous words start to pour out of his mouth. Then the dream fades.

My dream is a glimpse of the terror of being out of control. I am not aware of the test; in fact, I don't even know I'm supposed to be in class until I naively walk in and sit down. I have stumbled into a world where something is required of me, and I do not have what it takes to handle it. But I try, and although for a brief time I feel exhilarated with my activity, I am aware that my life is a counterfeit and I am eventually going to be found out. I feel powerless to tackle the weight of the burden placed on my shoulders.

In various ways, all of us feel helpless in a "big" person's world. Who makes the decision to keep us employed? In most cases, unless we own the company we are at the mercy of those we may not respect nor trust, but who nevertheless rule our financial future. Is it any better to own the company? If we own the company that produces a product or serves others, then we are controlled by the whim of the purchaser. Even those who appear to be in control are not.

My Algebra I dream is one variation on a common theme for many of us. It is a symbol of the hidden helplessness we face day to day. Our lives are a spectacle of helplessness. From birth to death we are bombarded by the presence and power of others. We are not free, at least not in the sense of being able to make choices that are unaffected by others. We are unable to break free of our culture, personal history, relationships, genetic makeup, or life's daily demands for basic survival.

The desire for control is only one side of the coin. The other side is a hatred of failure (personal death). My dream is a glimpse of the horror of failure. My incompetence is finally discovered and I am dragged to the front of the class. My work is evaluated and I am humiliated. The chaos of a cluster of papers floating about the teacher's desk is a symbol of disintegration: Failure will lead to humiliation and breakdown.

It feels like I can't win. The weeds of life seem destined to invade my garden. The harder I try to make life work, the more I seem to be assaulted from every side. When I decide to spend more time with the kids, something seems to spring out of the calendar to hinder my good intention. When I make a little extra money, the car breaks down. It is the second law of thermodynamics: entropy, decay, the rising tide of decline at work in every object, physical body, and relationship. It seems I am stuck with intermittent success, followed by the resurgence of more weeds.

We want control; we hate failure. The more we sense the possibility of personal or physical death, the greater our helplessness. Therefore, the more impotent we see ourselves, the greater our fear. Once our fears warn us that we are helpless, the only solution seems to be flight.

FEAR: THE RESPONSE OF FLIGHT

Fear is the strategy of flight: the flip side of anger. Both are responses to threat and danger. Anger attacks the threat; fear withdraws from it. Fear cringes before something or someone who might hurt us physically or psychologically. We respond in flight when we view the danger as being greater than our resources and determine that self-preservation is a higher good than engagement with the danger.

Fear serves a beneficial function in a fallen world. It warns us to take precautions, to hold back from certain people and situations. In this sense, fear operates analogously to pain. Pain warns us that something threatens damage to the body, and we recoil from it.

Without pain we would be in terrible shape. Think of being barefoot and stepping on something sharp like a tack. As soon as your foot touches the tack you jump to do whatever is necessary to remove it. If you didn't feel any pain, you wouldn't notice it was there until you happened to see it—and by that time infection might be setting in. The experience of pain isn't pleasant, but the alternative is much worse. It's the same with fear.

I (Tremper) enjoy exploring large cities. My work allows me to travel frequently, and when I go to a city and have some time I love to walk around exploring the urban landscape. I was recently in Chicago, one of my favorite cities. After visiting the Oriental Institute at the University of Chicago, I went downtown and parked. I began my afternoon adventure by visiting the Art Institute, then I strolled down Michigan Avenue for a while before cutting over to a restaurant area which includes the new Planet Hollywood.

After checking out Planet Hollywood I continued walking, but I soon began to feel anxious. Although it was still daylight, the deserted streets were getting narrower and dirtier. My sense of fear warned me to back off. This was not the place for me to wander alone, so I turned quickly around and went back to the well-traveled streets in the Loop.

Fear can function as a warning light when danger is near. It can function to keep ourselves from harm. However, it can go awry and often does.

THE DARK SIDE OF FEAR

Although withdrawal is frequently an appropriate response in a fallen world, fear can turn obsessive—clutching our hearts, inhibiting our activity and our enjoyment of God and His world. Instead of helping us, this kind of fear can cripple us.

For some, fear is so overwhelming that they cannot leave their house. These are extreme cases. However, many of us find that worry significantly holds us back from life.

Imprisoned in the Comfort Zone

Most of us live our lives within the boundaries of what is familiar and comfortable to us, in conditions that elicit the least anxiety. This is the comfort zone. Many of us are afraid to move out of it, because experiencing the new and unfamiliar often involves unpleasant feelings.

Of course, sometimes the tendency to stay in the comfort zone is beneficial, because it protects us from potential harm. My comfort zone keeps me from going ninety miles an hour on the freeway. These feelings of potential anxiety not only reduce the danger of an accident but save me considerable money in speeding fines.

Other times, however, staying within our zones of comfort can get us into trouble. On his first day of the eighth grade, my (Tremper's) usually unflappable son was reluctant to leave the warm protection of his home for the cold uncertainties of school. My wife and I spent an hour pulling him out of the comfort zone of his bed.

It's natural to want to keep problems at bay. But some people are so successful at putting up protective shields that they create a sheltered cocoon where nothing and nobody can touch them. In this case, fear no longer protects; it imprisons.

The Distorting Effects of Fear

Many strong emotions distort reality, but fear does so in particular ways. One of its distortions is a false perception of ourselves. We seem weaker than we really are, and more accountable as well. Generally, in the response of fear we tend to blame ourselves; in the response of anger we tend to blame others. In blaming ourselves, we gain the illusion of having control over some perceived failure that we feel we can and must change.

Fear also distorts our perception of the nature of the dangers facing us. If we think the threat is far beyond our ability to cope with it, then flight seems perfectly natural.

A friend related a story about his early ministry. Fresh out of seminary, Tom was learning the ropes with his first congregation and struggling a little with his preaching. One day a man called to schedule an appointment with him. Tom was elated that someone finally wanted his counsel.

At the scheduled time, the man showed up at Tom's office with seven tapes. "I'm not here to talk about me," he started right in. "I'm here to talk about you. Your preaching is killing us. Week after week we hear you drone on—you are going to destroy this church."

Tom barely had time to recover his senses before the man continued, "Take these seven tapes. Imitate the preacher's style. Your content is all right, I guess, but if you don't learn to deliver it the way Reverend Brown does, I shudder for the future of our church."

The next week was torture for Tom. On Sunday he stepped up to the pulpit to preach with a knot in his stomach and a dry mouth. He tried to maintain eye contact with the entire congregation, but it seemed that everywhere he looked he saw his critic's eyes glaring at him. "Everyone else's head was a normal size," Tom recalled, "but his seemed as big as a watermelon."

Fear distorts our sense of reality. Our enemies seem huge and all-powerful. Nowhere in the Bible is this expressed more vividly than in Isaiah 30:17:

> A thousand will flee
>   at the threat of one;
> at the threat of five
>   you will all flee away,
> till you are left
>   like a flagstaff on a mountaintop,
>   like a banner on a hill.

The enemy seems overwhelming; we seem weak, inadequate, and alone. And God? He is nowhere to be found. Tom could have said with the psalmist:

> Many bulls surround me;
>   strong bulls of Bashan encircle me.
> Roaring lions that tear their prey
>   open their mouths wide against me.
> *Psalm 22:12-13*

Tom's fear not only distorted reality, but it also created the very reality he was trying to avoid: his inability to speak authoritatively and persuasively to his congregation. His fear choked off whatever ability he had to communicate.

As with all strong emotions, fear can consume our minds. In the world of opera, a "leitmotif" is a dominant tune or musical phrase that recurs throughout the whole work. Our minds often operate that way. Our fearful thoughts recur until they dominate our thinking. What is the key to controlling them?

THE KEY TO OUR STRUGGLE WITH FEAR

Laura spoke in a hush: "In the quiet moments at the end of the day, when you're not thinking of what must be done, when your mind is not filled with activity and noise, do you feel pleasure or do you feel fear?"

Therapists often avoid answering direct questions. The firm intensity of her eyes and the commanding power of her voice compelled me (Dan) to answer. "More often than not," I admitted, "I feel nothing but exhaustion."

Her glance was intense: "I feel fear when exhaustion has taken away my ability to remain numb."

Her suffering had taught her that exhaustion does not hide feeling—it strips away the facade of balance and the pretense of control. Her husband, a good man, had recently died at forty-three. She was now single in a world of couples.

To make matters worse, Jim had not kept his insurance current. Two years prior to his death, a business deal had sapped all their extra money. Without her knowledge, Jim had canceled his major life insurance policy. It was a stupid mistake; he had simply forgotten to renew it once finances improved. But his failure was a terrible blow. She was going to lose her house and a private education for her kids, and she would be forced back to work far sooner than she felt was good for the family.

In her quiet moments of dread, however, the real pain had little to do with the tough realities she faced. She felt betrayed by her dead husband. Why hadn't he consulted with her about canceling the policy? The answer seemed simple—he had not wanted to deal with her questions and fears. He had apparently chosen the easy way out for himself, and his cowardice was an assault as painful as his death. She felt cold anger that floated to fear when she thought about how she was going to handle the days ahead.

What could I say to her that might help her struggle with her fear? It would seem cruel and insensitive simply to counsel her, "Don't be afraid." But that seems to be what the Scriptures offer:

> Though an army besiege me,
>   my heart will not fear;
> though war break out against me,
>   even then I will be confident.
> *Psalm 27:3*

> Therefore we will not fear, though the earth give way
>   and the mountains fall into the heart of the sea,
> though its waters roar and foam
>   and the mountains quake with their surging.
> *Psalm 46:2-3*

> Say to those with fearful hearts,
>   "Be strong, do not fear;
> your God will come,
>   he will come with vengeance;
> with divine retribution
>   he will come to save you."
> *Isaiah 35:4*

> So do not fear, for I am with you;
>   do not be dismayed, for I am your God.

I will strengthen you and help you;
    I will uphold you with my righteous right hand.
Isaiah 41:10

The Spirit you received does not make you slaves, so
that you live in fear again; rather, the Spirit you received
brought about your adoption to sonship. And by him
we cry, "*Abba*, Father."
Romans 8:15

There is no fear in love. But perfect love drives out fear,
because fear has to do with punishment. The one who
fears is not made perfect in love.
1 John 4:18

How are we to understand this counsel? Are the biblical writers
simply insensitive to the realities of living in a fallen world? Their
answer to fear seems to be, *Don't.* Is it really that simple?

There's no getting away from the reality that fear is basic to human
existence. But the counsel of Scripture indicates that resolving our
fear requires us to struggle with our deepest allegiance: It all boils
down not to *whether* we fear, but *what and whom* we fear.

7

Constructive Fear:
The Fear of the Lord

One summer evening my son Andrew and I (Tremper) left home to pick up a take-out order for pizza. The skies were cloudy, but we didn't give it much thought because we hadn't heard any warnings, and severe weather is rare in the Philadelphia area.

When we got to the restaurant, lightning struck and the lights went out. We hurriedly got our pizza and ran to the car. As we began the ten-minute drive back to our house, the wind really picked up. We turned onto a road that was at the bottom of a small gully just in time to witness a huge tree falling right in front of the car, bringing electrical wires down with it.

We cautiously turned the car around, only to be stunned by yet another huge tree crashing right in front of us, straddling the gully. After recovering my senses I realized that at any moment another tree might fall, this time right on top of the car.

I discovered that our car could just barely make its way under the second large tree trunk, and we escaped from the gully. The rest of the way home, which normally would take three minutes, took us an hour and a half as we cut through the debris left by the tornado that had hit our neighborhood.

The threats we face often entail very real dangers. A routine drive to pick up a pizza had turned into two harrowing hours of life-and-death terror. Fear is not abnormal. In fact, to live without fear is to be inhuman.

We cannot escape fear, but we can allow it to move us to a deeper comprehension of what it means to exist before God. Once we have acknowledged the realities of our fears, how do we allow them to drive us toward God? The psalmist, who experienced the same level of intense fear as we do, shows us how.

FEAR: THE DIRECTION OF OUR FLIGHT

In the course of his prayer to the Lord in Psalm 55, David describes the condition of his heart:

> My heart is in anguish within me;
>   the terrors of death have fallen on me.
> Fear and trembling have beset me;
>   horror has overwhelmed me.
>
> *Psalm 55:4-5*

The danger that confronts him has seized his mind with such obsessive fury that he can think of nothing else. Both internally ("My heart") and externally ("trembling"), he shows his severe anxiety.

All his impulses tell him to flee the danger. He uses an image that combines two elements in order to communicate his desired flight.

74

I said, "Oh, that I had the wings of a dove!
    I would fly away and be at rest.
I would flee far away
    and stay in the desert;
I would hurry to my place of shelter,
    far from the tempest and storm."
Psalm 55:6-8

David desires to be a bird, specifically a dove. From a human perspective, birds are skittish. They (urban pigeons excepted) do not tolerate a foreign, threatening presence; as soon as they sense threat, they take flight. They are fast, and their ability to soar to the heights allows them to bypass obstacles on the ground.

The dove, well known in Israel, often nested in the crevices of cliffs, away from the chaos of the city. Such cliffs were found in the Israelite wilderness (a better translation of the Hebrew than the NIV's "desert"), an area between the city and the absolutely barren desert. There was enough sustenance for a bird to live on, but it was away from city-threat.

In the psalmist, fear evokes a desire to flee. What has caused this terror? David does not specify. Though there certainly was a very specific situation that provoked him to compose this psalm, he hides the details so that the lessons can be transposed to other individuals' particular circumstances. Indeed, when he first describes the threat he speaks generically of an enemy:

I see violence and strife in the city.
Day and night they prowl about on its walls;
    malice and abuse are within it.
Destructive forces are at work in the city;
    threats and lies never leave its streets.
Psalm 55:9-11

One very significant detail is cited in the next section, however, which makes David's fear all the more incomprehensible to him. He can't believe it, but behind it all was a friend!

> If an enemy were insulting me,
>   I could endure it;
> if a foe were rising against me,
>   I could hide.
> But it is you, a man like myself,
>   my companion, my close friend,
> with whom I once enjoyed sweet fellowship
>   at the house of God,
> as we walked about
>   among the worshipers.
> *Psalm 55:12-14*

What insult added to injury! Someone he trusted had brutally betrayed him in a life-threatening way. We cannot be sure what actual historical situation is reflected in this psalm, but it does sound similar to the events that surrounded the rebellion of Absalom against David.

At that time the kingdom was torn in half. It is hard to imagine David's emotions at this low point in his life, when friend and child turned against him. One such friend and close companion was Ahithophel, the wise man, who turned against David and offered his advice to Absalom (see 2 Samuel 15:30-31; 16:15–17:23). We don't get enough detail in the psalm or the historical books to be sure, but the situation was similar, if not identical. A close friend had violated David's trust and hurt him badly:

> My companion attacks his friends;
>   he violates his covenant.
> His talk is smooth as butter,
>   yet war is in his heart;

his words are more soothing than oil,
>   yet they are drawn swords.
Psalm 55:20-21

The enemy is a murderous hypocrite. David's desire is to flee far away from danger. And he does take flight, according to the final part of his prayer-psalm—but not to the wilderness. Instead, he flees to God. After acknowledging his fears, he turns to God and lays out his problems before Him.

That's what this psalm is all about. It is a lament prayer, a lengthy petition and complaint before the Lord. A prayer that he knows God hears:

Evening, morning and noon
>   I cry out in distress,
>   and he hears my voice.
Psalm 55:17

David knows that God will respond to his fears by His divine presence, which saves His people and destroys His enemies. And who are His enemies? They are the ones who "have no fear of God" (verse 19).

A CHANGE OF HEART:
FROM FEAR OF THE WORLD TO FEAR OF GOD

Not All Fear Is Sinful

Many Christians are reluctant to admit they are afraid because they believe that their fears are inherently sinful.

But remember Jesus in the garden of Gethsemane. Alluding to Psalm 43:5, He said to the disciples, "My soul is overwhelmed with sorrow to the point of death. Stay here and keep watch with me" (Matthew 26:38). As Jesus confronted not only the reality of His approaching death but also the tremendous burden of sin that He was taking on His soul, He was filled with deep dread.

Let us be careful not to spiritualize away the depth of Christ's fear. He was man. He was God. He knew from the foundation of the universe that He would become flesh and bear the penalty of His creation's rebellion. Yet He pleaded to escape the horror of His Father's assault and abandonment, praying that "this cup be taken from me."

The cup Jesus referred to here is the "cup of wrath," which is mentioned in a number of places in the Old Testament, including the Psalms:

> In the hand of the LORD is a cup
>> full of foaming wine mixed with spices;
> he pours it out, and all the wicked of the earth
>> drink it down to its very dregs.
> *Psalm 75:8*

Since Jesus took upon Himself the sins of the world, He had to drink from the cup of God's wrath—the very wrath that sent Him to the cross on our behalf. Out of fear and trepidation, Jesus was asking to escape the cross. But almost in the same breath, He agreed to do what His Father wanted of Him. After the internal struggle in the garden, He stepped out toward the cross without looking back.

Jesus was fully God as well as fully human, and therefore vulnerable to all the temptations that we are, but without sin. So when we see Jesus in the garden "sweating blood" as He anticipated death by crucifixion, it is possible to be afraid without sinning (see also Hebrews 2:14-18; 4:14-16).

Where Does Fear Drive Us?

Where do we cross the line from a legitimate fear of a dangerous world to a fear that not only imprisons us but also offends God?

It has to do with *what or whom we fear*. And where does that fear drive us? Does it drive us to protect ourselves, or does it drive us to God, our Protector?

Jesus did not fear human beings. Neither did He fear excruciating physical pain. He feared the loss, the assault, the anger, the rejection of His Father: Jesus feared God.

Oddly, it is the fear of the world that drives us away from God. Fear of God strips away all other fears and compels us to deal with God, transcendent and infinitely higher than any mere mortal fear. Fear of God roots us not in our problems but in the essence of existence.

Jesus' fear in the garden drove Him to His Father. He chose His Father's will because He—though God Himself—submitted Himself in service to His Father. He took the apparently irrational route to the cross and death.

The Fear of the Lord

The Psalms, and the Bible generally, extol a type of fear that God greatly desires to instill in us. It is the fear of the Lord. "The LORD delights in those who fear him, who put their hope in his unfailing love" (Psalm 147:11).

Fear distorts our perception of ourselves so that we seem weaker than we really are. It distorts the size of our problems so that they seem huge and undefeatable. But perhaps most significantly, *fear distorts our picture of God*. God seems weak, uninvolved, or uncaring in the midst of our troubles. *After all*, we think, *if He were strong and concerned, He would not leave us in this mess.*

Fear reverses reality by making evil seem all-conquering, and God impotent. But God is not impotent. The Psalms bombard us with images of His power. He is a king (Psalm 47), a warrior (18:7-15), a rock (31:2), and a fortress (46:7, 11). They also fill our minds with pictures of His goodness, compassion, and mercy. He is a shepherd (Psalm 23) and a loving mother (Psalm 131).

God is not impotent; and, in one sense, neither are we, as long as the direction of our existence expresses our heart to serve Him. We are impotent to keep our children from making harmful choices, but we can let their sin draw us to wrestle with God and ultimately bow before Him.

When our sight is blurred by the effects of fear, however, how do we get our orientation back? How do we regain a sense of reality when the threats seem so real and the dangers so present?

The answer boils down to *feel fear*. If you avoid your fear, it will turn dark and destructive. Instead, allow it to stalk you without trying to wave it away by reciting pious platitudes or distracting yourself in busyness. Fear faced is a heart exposed. The stronger the fear, the greater the clarity regarding the object of our fear.

Fear clarifies by exposing whom (and what) we serve. It can be classified in two categories: *fear of the world* or *fear of God*. Fear of the world always relates to the potential death of our agenda—to create a world as close to Eden as possible. Most of our fears arise out of our demand to gain a degree of pleasure, honor, meaning, and joy in a world that more often hands us pain, shame, chaos, and sorrow. The fear of the world is another way of describing the fear of what life—of what others—may do to me.

What does it mean, instead, to fear God?

"The fear of the LORD is the beginning of wisdom," declares the psalmist; "all who follow his precepts have good understanding" (Psalm 111:10). Some people emaciate this truth by insisting that this word does not really mean "fear"; it means only "hold in awe" or "revere." After all, the thinking goes, God—to whom we have continuous access—is our best friend; Jesus is a "friend of sinners." Therefore, there's no need to be afraid of our good buddy God.

However, exclusive emphasis on these truths about God robs us of the comfort of knowing that God is also the Creator, the One who sustains the entire universe; the Judge who determines who lives and who dies, who goes to heaven and who goes to hell. He is a being so far above our thoughts that we cannot even fathom Him.

Our rather sappy, sentimental Christianity does not allow us to experience the power behind Jesus' words: "I tell you, my friends, do not be afraid of those who kill the body and after that can do no more. But I will show you whom you should fear: Fear him who, after your body has been killed, has authority to throw you into hell. Yes, I tell you, fear him" (Luke 12:4-5).

Human beings and the forces of creation can kill only our bodies. God can kill our bodies, but, even worse, He can destroy us by utterly separating Himself from us. This is hell—a darkness so thick and chaotic that nothing of His glory redeems and enlivens the soul. I am to fear the utter loss of my self in the radical loss of God.

Even David pleaded with God, "Do not cast me from your presence or take your Holy Spirit from me" (Psalm 51:11). He was terrified at the thought that God would toss him away and remove His presence from his soul. Some might consign this terror to an Old Testament view of God, which we are now free to put behind us. But Jesus, in the following parable, seems to imply that we ought to be equally concerned:

> Then the man who had received one bag of gold came.
> "Master," he said, "I knew that you are a hard man,
> harvesting where you have not sown and gathering where
> you have not scattered seed. So I was afraid and went out
> and hid your gold in the ground. See, here is what belongs
> to you."
>
> His master replied, "You wicked, lazy servant! So you
> knew that I harvest where I have not sown and gather where
> I have not scattered seed? . . .
>
> "Take the bag of gold from him and give it to the one
> who has ten bags. For whoever who has will be given more,

and they will have an abundance. Whoever does not have, even what they have will be taken from them. And throw that worthless servant outside, into the darkness, where there will be weeping and gnashing of teeth."
Matthew 25:24-26, 28-30

This parable is not about whether we sin greatly, or struggle with severe problems, or if we are actively engaged in formal ministry. It has to do with preparation. Are we anxious, anticipating, and prepared for His return? The prepared and wise heart lives with a hope, an ear to the wind, and an eye to the horizon for the Master's return.

To fear God is to know that a moment of existence without Him is hell. We can live in various degrees of distance from Him—each step away is a foot closer to the dark hollow of hell. We are to fear the loss of existence; we are to fear the loss of the very essence of humanness as we walk on the edge of rebellion.

Further, to fear God is to be stunned speechless that the weight of His fury and rejection crushed His Son, not us. Awe is not appreciation; it is stone-cold terror at the sense of otherness. Most human parents would kill in an instant any who tried to harm their child. Not God: He killed His Son to make the depths of His glory known.

We think of God as being radically other in His omniscience, omnipotence, and omnipresence. Indeed, He is. But He is most radically other in His love. To fear God is to fear His intense, radically other-centered love. Perfect love casts out fear, because that kind of love is more frightening than any fear of earthly harm. We are terrified of love—we should be, because it is so alien and unknown.

What does it mean to fear God? It means to be anxious and eager to greet Him. It means to build our lives around the call of being His bride, to anticipate the pleasure of love and the aroma of passion. To fear God is to be consumed with His presence.

If we fear God, how can we fear the vain efforts of human beings and worldly institutions? After all, big fears make little fears go away. Our life might be filled with fears about a multitude of daily circumstances, but if a doctor suddenly announced that we had only six months to live due to inoperable cancer, all those daily fears would melt away before the news.

God is the One we should fear most of all. When we disorient ourselves by being less afraid of God than something else, we get into trouble. When we fear something else, we forget about fearing God. This is what happened to the Israelites who lived during the time of Isaiah, so that God had to confront them by saying:

> Whom have you so dreaded and feared
>> that you have not been true to me,
> and have neither remembered me
>> nor taken this to heart?
> Is it not because I have long been silent
>> that you do not fear me?
>
> *Isaiah 57:11*

In God's presence, all human fears disappear like smoke dispersed by the wind.

C. S. Lewis pictures the fear of God in his classic Narnia tale *The Lion, the Witch and the Wardrobe.* Mr. and Mrs. Beaver are describing to Lucy and Peter the one who can rescue Narnia from evil and danger: a lion named Aslan. Lucy is not so sure that she's ready to meet such a dangerous creature and asks if he's safe. "Safe?" Mr. Beaver reacts. "Don't you hear what Mrs. Beaver tells you? Who said anything about safe? 'Course he isn't safe. But he's good. He's the King, I tell you."[1]

Too often, we let the fear of the world drive us into ourselves, where we find no strength. Instead, we should let it drive us to the fear of God. The fear of God does not drive us away from God, but rather to God. It is only as the fear of God overcomes our fear of the world that we can truly and productively cope with our fears in the world.

Fear is flight away from harm. It is the product of helplessness, weakness brought about by a feeling of inadequacy and lack of control. If we demand control and success, we will be destroyed, because in a sinful world our weaknesses will continually be exposed. But if we submit to God instead of demanding control, and serve God instead of insisting on success, then we will be changed, and our fears will dissipate. God's sovereignty is the ultimate issue as we face this choice. If we clutch desperately for success and control, we deny His power. If we exercise the privilege of submission and service, we acknowledge it.

Let's pick up on Tom's story, the pastor who was afraid of his congregation, from chapter 6. It didn't end with his fear from the pulpit of the parishioner who told him that his preaching was killing the church. Tom had a significant encounter after that service.

As Tom was standing by the door, going through the torture of greeting the departing members of his congregation, the last person to leave was an elderly woman. She came up to him with a stern expression on her face and said, "I don't know who has gotten to you, Tom. But you are preaching to please someone in the congregation. I want you to go back to your study immediately and repent. Then I want you to prepare your sermon for next week in such a way as to seek to please God, not whomever you were preaching for today!"

He was struck by the truth of her comments. He had let the fear of this man overwhelm his fear of God. He did as she so wisely instructed. It was one thing to let this one man down—even his whole church—he realized, but it was quite another to disappoint the God of the universe. Thus his terrible fear of his critic faded away before his fear of God.

THE PROCESS OF CHANGE

To allow God to transform our fearfulness, we must first *acknowledge our fears.* This means resisting the impulse to act as if they weren't there, deadening our strong feelings through busyness in distracting activities. That was the route taken by Theresa, the mother who worried about her son Robert but tried to shove her worry out of her mind by running to the next meeting.

Second, we must *struggle with our worry.* This is in contrast to the philosophy that advocates, "simply trust Jesus and your worries will disappear." Once you acknowledge your fears, you're in for a real battle. It's only after struggle that you will experience lasting peace (see Psalm 131).

Third, through Scripture and prayer, *remember God's power and His marvelous acts of past help.* Begin with Scripture, where we confront the astonishing nature of God. Time and again the Bible records God's work in history to save His people from incredible dangers. You might also remember testimonies that you have heard from friends or in church. But most important, remember how God has worked over the years in your own life. He did it in the past; He can do it in the present.

Then, finally, with the confidence that you have gained, move out into the world. At first, the process may be slow and painful. You may feel great pressure to retreat to a safe place where there is no hurt. But keep in mind that the safe places, those with no hurt, are also places with no joy.

The fear of God overwhelms the fear of the world.

8

Dark Desire:
Envy and Jealousy

Robert lay on his stomach and tried to breathe rhythmically. He was afraid to move. His wife, Nancy, tossed and turned in bed, obviously trying to get his attention. Perhaps he could keep her from noticing that he was awake. He knew he should talk to her, but it was the middle of the night and he was exhausted. He would make a point to speak to her in the morning . . .

"Robert, are you awake?"

Oh, well, no escaping now. "Yes, honey—what's wrong?"

"I'm worried about Sarah."

"Can this wait until morning? It's only three o'clock."

"But I can't sleep," Nancy complained. "I'm so worried."

They had had this conversation many times before—usually in the middle of the night—about Sarah, their eighteen-year-old daughter who was deciding on a college for next year.

"I just wish that she had made better choices along the way,"

Nancy went on. "Then she would have had early acceptance to Wake Forest, and she wouldn't have to worry so much now."

"She had to focus on her studies, honey," Robert pointed out. "She got great grades, better than you or I did. She'll get in somewhere she likes."

. "I don't know whether she will or not. Her grades aren't that much better than ours, and we had to settle for the Ogden extension of State."

Robert grimaced internally. He had heard this a number of times before, and it always hurt. Sure, Ogden wasn't high on the prestige meter, but they had met each other there. Also, the education led right to the job he loved so much. He said nothing.

His wife continued, "It seems so unfair that her friend Katey got in. Her grades weren't nearly as good as Sarah's. She just had all those extracurricular activities. If only Sarah could have played a sport or joined the chess club."

"Nancy, come on, I can hardly keep my eyes open, and we've been through this a hundred times. Sarah couldn't kick a soccer ball straight if her life depended on it. And she didn't have time to play chess on top of taking her advanced math class. You know we encouraged her to spend whatever little extra time she had with her youth group. Katey didn't have that problem. She could use Sunday mornings to catch up on her studies. Please, Nancy, let's go back to sleep now. I've got to be at the airport by eight . . ."

OUR DESIRE FOR POSSESSION

As humans, we have a few basic needs: a minimal amount of water, a modicum of food, and enough shelter to keep us from freezing to death. We can survive on very little.

But the vast majority of humanity wants to do more than simply survive. We desire to live comfortably, even well. We crave a variety of tastes to slake our thirst: lemonades, colas, flavored waters, and more. We want enough food to fill—and expand—our stomachs. And we want a lot more than mere shelter; we desire bigger and better homes.

Necessities are not all we want, of course. We desire all sorts of material things—cars, clothes, books, jewelry, Jacuzzis, ski vacations. Once again, the basic item is not enough. If I have a Timex watch, I long for a Rolex. If I drive a Hyundai, I've got my eye on a Mercedes. And all of us desire money, which, in our world, makes possession possible.

Not all our desires are for material goods, however. If it weren't for the fact that some people have survived long periods of time alone, we might classify relationships as a basic need along with water, food, and shelter. We want to be with people we know well and who enjoy being with us. We long for close, fully satisfying relationships.

Our desires consistently extend beyond our needs. But we live in a world with limited resources, and the universe is not equitable. Some people have greater pleasure, greater wealth, greater power, and greater joy in relationships than others. In short, we are finite and so are the resources. Two words describe the attendant feelings in our desire for possession: *envy* and *jealousy*.

RESENTFUL DESIRE—ENVY

Envy is the desire for what another has that we don't have. It is a resentful desire. In our consumer-oriented society, envy grasps at another person's material possessions or personal status. But envy can be much more subtle, even appearing with a good face, in the desire for relationships that we see others enjoying.

We may be tempted to justify envy if we're desiring something on behalf of someone else—such as Nancy's wish that her daughter Sarah had been admitted to a big-name school. Although it's likely that Nancy was genuinely concerned for Sarah's future, she was also—and perhaps primarily—projecting her own frustrated desires onto her daughter. The combination led to insomnia and internal conflict.

Nancy's envy was physically upsetting. The expression "green with envy" reminds us that extreme envy can produce symptoms similar to nausea. The same is true with jealousy.

A DESIRE TO PROTECT—JEALOUSY

In contrast to envy, a resentful desire for what another person has, jealousy is a desire to protect what we do have (or falsely assume that we possess) and which we fear another may take away from us. It results in hypervigilance and hoarding.

When we think of jealousy, we think especially of male-female relationships—the stuff of movies and soap operas. But it is also the stuff of real life, in all relationships.

A friend confided that he felt uneasy about how much time his wife spent with another man at work. Their jobs required them to work in the office together, eat dinner with clients often, and even travel to other cities occasionally. His wife seemed to enjoy it a little too much. But he loved her and trusted her, and he felt constrained by the Bible's teaching in 1 Corinthians 13:7 that "love always trusts." He felt guilty about his jealous feelings, which cropped up too often for him to feel that he was coping successfully with them.

Jealousy is not restricted to intimate male-female relationships, however. Another friend subtly restricts his son's relationships with other adults. He has a good relationship with his son, does a lot with him, and is jealous of his time with him. On the excuse that the family is so busy, he does not encourage his son to get involved with the youth group at church, and especially the youth leader, who has shown interest in getting to know his son. All the publicity about sexual abuse of young boys gives him a rationale for not letting his son go anywhere alone with an adult, whether a coach, youth leader, Scout troop leader, or minister.

In fact, jealousy occurs in virtually any type of intimate human relationship. Threesomes are particularly susceptible. I (Tremper) attended a three-day meeting during which three of us made a number of important decisions concerning a new translation of the Bible. One morning I noticed that I was growing irritated with my colleagues, whom I had known for some time and liked very much. They had been agreeing together against me for about an hour. I was ready to explode with indignation that they were constantly changing my translation ("after all," I reasoned "they're just stylists, and I'm the expert on Hebrew").

I soon realized, however, that my professional expertise was not the issue, but rather my fear that I was left outside of the relationship. I was jealous of their friendship, which at that point seemed to be excluding me.

Although jealousy is most often associated with relationships, it can also be applied to things. The unique character of jealousy in contrast to envy is not things versus relationships, but a desire to hold on to what one has, to the exclusion of others, versus a desire to acquire what someone else possesses.

Michael is a theologian with a large library. He has taken care to amass an outstanding private collection of books—almost as if the number of books he owns in some way reflects his intelligence. In fact, he has so many books that he can't possibly use them all; many of them go unread.

When Michael's students and colleagues cannot locate a book in the school's library, they don't even consider asking Michael to lend them his copy. They've asked before, but Michael has consistently turned them down, citing his fear that they might lose the book. Those who know him, however, suspect that he is less concerned to protect the books than he is to safeguard the reputation of his intellect.

PSALM 73: GREEN WITH DESIRE

As we turn to the Psalms, the mirror of our soul, once again we discover that the psalmist precedes us in all of our emotions, including dark desire.

In one of the most emotionally intense prayers in the book of Psalms, Asaph shares his feelings of envy toward those who seem to have more than he does: "I envied the arrogant when I saw the prosperity of the wicked" (73:3). He goes on to describe the carefree and successful life of the godless people around him:

> They have no struggles;
>   their bodies are healthy and strong.
> They are free from common human burdens;
>   they are not plagued by human ills. . . .
> This is what the wicked are like—
>   always free of care, they go on amassing wealth.
> *Psalm 73:4-5, 12*

Envy had distorted reality for the psalmist. The target of his envy, the wealthy wicked, had taken on superhuman qualities in his mind. We observed in chapter 6 that fear makes others seem more powerful and ourselves weaker. Here we can see how resentful desire distorts reality by making other people appear better off, richer, happier than they really are, and ourselves worse off, poorer, sadder.

There is a reality behind the distortion, however. The fabulously rich are insulated from some of the problems afflicting the rest of us. Their money permits them to spend more time on exercise, tanning sessions, and vacations. In one magazine interview, a wealthy woman was asked how she had succeeded in losing so much weight within a month. She casually responded, "Anyone can do it. I just committed myself to a three-hour daily workout." The letters that poured in afterward indicated that few could afford even ten minutes in the midst of an occupation, child-rearing, and the general wear and tear of life. The rich can afford to hire maids, gardeners, au pairs, cooks, even chauffeurs—and thus avoid many of the energy-draining hassles that the rest of humanity must endure.

If you're not wealthy, you must slave away to make ends meet. After working a long day, you come home and nuke dinner in the microwave. Then it's time to fold laundry and later fall exhausted into bed. Imagine flipping on the television for a moment's escape, only to see "Lifestyles of the Rich and Famous." As you hear Robin Leech's arrogant-sounding accent while he walks the beaches of South America or attends the opening of a mega-resort in Asia, you turn green. If you're honest, you'll admit with Asaph, "I envied the arrogant."

ENVY AND JEALOUSY: FROM ANNOYANCE TO OBSESSION

As with all emotions, we experience envy and jealousy at different levels of intensity. Watching a neighbor turn into his driveway in his high-priced BMW may make us slightly uncomfortable as we think of our old Buick that's pushing 150,000 miles on the odometer. But dark desire can capture our hearts when resentment is overtaken by hate.

King Saul's relationship with David illustrates this escalation (see 1 Samuel 16–19). When the two first met, Saul loved the young shepherd boy. David's music calmed the king's soul, and his bravery in fighting the Philistine giant Goliath rid Israel of a great external threat (chapter 17).

But Saul had position; he was the first king of Israel. As he compared David's abilities to his own, he grew jealous. More frightening than David's greater abilities was the fact that Saul had been disobedient to God, and God's presence had left him.

Saul's jealousy became obsessive. When he heard the popular song being chanted in the streets, "Saul has slain his thousands, and David his tens of thousands," he was provoked to hypervigilance: "From that time on Saul kept a jealous eye on David" (1 Samuel 18:9).

Saul recognized David's bright gifts and courage; he knew his own lack and failure. And he could not bear this discrepancy of gifts and calling. His desire to protect his kingship escalated his feelings toward David from affection, to annoyance, to murderous obsession. He was blinded by his furious desires.

BLIND AMBITION

Ambition is a strong desire to possess something. The object may be material, such as money, or intangible, such as celebrity or power.

Many of us distance ourselves from ambitious desires for money, fame, or power, ascribing them to the self-aggrandizers who will do anything to possess them. Celebrity! Entertainment stars may struggle with it, but it's another world to me. Power! Politicians and heads of major corporations might be prey to its lure, but I live in the ordinary world.

When we think this way, however, we avoid the darker recesses of our hearts. The fame that my ambition seeks might not be worldwide adulation as much as credit for my particular achievements in my world. I might not seek power over a whole city, state, or country, but I might long to control a colleague, a family member, or a friend. Ambition is not inherently evil, but it can merge with envy or jealousy to produce a ruthless drive to consume everything in its way. This ambition is often called "blind" because it ignores those who are crushed on its way to achieving its aim.

The teacher in the book of Ecclesiastes rightly recognized that society is often motivated by an envy-fueled ambition: "And I saw that all toil and all achievement spring from one person's envy of another" (Ecclesiastes 4:4). This observation so angered the frustrated Teacher that he concluded once again that the world is meaningless.

Such cruel ambition affects even the supposedly sacrosanct halls of our society today. The seminary where I (Tremper) teach is widely regarded as one of the best in the country, attracting fine, intelligent, godly students from over thirty countries. It is also an intense environment that demands academic excellence from students who must frequently work on the side to support their families, remain active in their local churches, and survive in an urban environment.

Last year, in a course on the prophet Zechariah, students were preparing for a test on the Hebrew of that biblical book. One week before the test, a crucial research book, necessary to prepare for the exam, was vandalized. Someone had taken a razor blade and cut out the relevant pages.

More was intended here than simply the procurement of a copy of the material to study at home, because all students had opportunity to photocopy the pages for a very small cost. The only conclusion was that someone wanted to prevent others from studying the book, so that his grade would stand out.

The perpetrator was never caught. But concern rippled through the seminary community over the irony of envious ambition in the context of preparing leaders for ministry.

THE FURY OF POSSESSION

Envy, jealousy, and blind ambition are all symptoms of a desire to possess that is fueled by rage. We cannot bear the prospect of losing something we consider essential to our well-being. The threat to our desires seems to threaten the quality of life—even life itself.

Jealousy is a desire to protect our beloved possession from alien suitors. Envy is a desire to acquire or repossess the jewel of our eye. When they escalate to possessive fury, they become destructive.

THE CRY OF THE SOUL

This is the irony of these dark desires: They actually destroy what we want. The decade of the eighties contains numerous illustrations of ambition taken to extremes—epitomized by names such as Boesky, Helmsley, and Milikin. They desired money, power, celebrity, and they let neither people nor laws stand in their way. For a flash, they were on top—they owned fabulous homes, drove expensive cars, and were recognized wherever they went. Where are they now? Jail. Their ambition destroyed them.

Asaph recognized this phenomenon. He knew that the success of the wicked was short-lived, and that his own envy could in the end destroy him: "But as for me, my feet had almost slipped; I had nearly lost my foothold" (73:2). After struggling with his envy, he concluded that evil people were only apparently well-off. God could ruin them at any time:

> Surely you place them on slippery ground;
>   you cast them down to ruin.
> How suddenly are they destroyed,
>   completely swept away by terrors!
> They are like a dream when one awakes;
>   when you arise, Lord,
> you will despise them as fantasies.
> *Psalm 73:18-20*

This is not to say that every envious person who becomes rich through devious means will die poor. But Asaph had developed a long-range vision of God's justice. He reached peace with his God when he realized:

> Yet I am always with you;
>   you hold me by my right hand.

96

You guide me with your counsel,
    and afterward you will take me into glory.
Whom have I in heaven but you?
    And earth has nothing I desire besides you.
My flesh and my heart may fail,
    but God is the strength of my heart
    and my portion forever.
Those who are far from you will perish;
    you destroy all who are unfaithful to you.
But as for me, it is good to be near God.
    I have made the Sovereign LORD my refuge;
    I will tell of all your deeds.

Psalm 73:23-28

The vision of divine justice put Asaph back on his feet. It refocused his heart to see all other desires as insignificant in light of knowing God.

Does this change in perspective imply that Asaph lost all desire for earthly things or people? Sadly, many assume that the more we mature, the less we desire. In fact, the more we grow, the more we hunger for what only heaven can provide. And yet earthly tastes, senses, and passions provide a picture of the ultimate redemption of all things. To desire heaven is not to desire earth less; it is to desire earth so deeply that it draws our heart to an anticipation of ecstasy in the light of God's embrace.

To vilify all desire in order to overcome envy and jealousy is a false solution. There is a place in our lives for intense desire. The Buddhist tradition, not the Christian tradition, affirms striving to relinquish all worldly desire.

In Christian teaching, the world is not a mirage but a reality that God created "good." There is a place for ambition for excellence.

The psalmist, for example, prides himself in his zeal (Psalm 69:9). Even a strong desire for possession can be good and noble. Indeed, desire motivates people to pursue and achieve excellence in those areas in which God has called them to serve. A world without desire would produce lives of unrelieved mediocrity—as if we'd all had a lobotomy. Desire that is devoid of resentment, and ambition that is respectful of others, prompt people to work in such a way as to bring glory to God.

Nevertheless, ever since early Christian times, the nonbiblical ideal of bland complacency has crept into the church. In a church influenced by Greek philosophy, a false dichotomy of body and spirit led to the exaltation of chastity and poverty. The monastic movement capitalized in part on a view of spirituality that censured all desires, except for religious ones, as evil and sinful. Even today, some preach satisfaction in Jesus to the point of mediocrity—as if investing one's gifts and energy in a profession is tantamount to craving the rewards of this world.

What is the difference between holy ambition and fleshly yearning? It is simply this: *what we seek to possess* and *whom we seek to serve*.

Earthly desire strives to possess, hoard, and defend against hunger, uncertainty, and injustice, as if there were no God—or at least no God worthy of our worship.

Heavenly desire strives not to possess, but to create—reflecting the Creator's glory in works of beauty and excellence. It seeks not to hoard, but to give; not to protect personal status, but to bless.

Why is this godly desire so rare in our business, political, academic, creative, and religious communities? Why is earthly envy and jealousy the norm? The scarcity can be traced to a universal human condition. At their core, envy and destructive jealousy arise from the perception of loss or the fear of abandonment—especially the abandonment of God.

WHERE IS GOD?

All of us experience envy and jealousy in our lives. But few of us allow the horizontal experience of envy and jealousy to raise the vertical question, *Where is God?* God, after all, is all-powerful. He can do anything. Not only that, He claims to love us. So why does He seem to abandon us to loss, loneliness, and disappointment?

Why does one couple who has spent years praying for a child and spending thousands of dollars for fertility drugs come up empty? Why do their neighbors, who disdain everything religious, have a beautiful little daughter? This discrepancy is the breeding ground for jealousy and misgivings about God's goodness. The psalmist articulates this feeling:

> In his pride the wicked man does not seek him;
> in all his thoughts there is no room for God.
> His ways are always prosperous;
> your laws are rejected by him;
> he sneers at all his enemies.
>
> *Psalm 10:4-5*

At one point, Asaph almost threw up his hands and rejected God because he felt that godliness did nothing for him: "Surely in vain I have kept my heart pure and have washed my hands in innocence" (73:13).

If God is the Creator of the entire cosmos, who controls all things, then why do the arrogant prosper while the godly suffer? Why did Asaph live poorly while his godless enemies thrived? Why does God give gifts to those who care nothing about Him while He lets those who love Him merely eke out an existence?

These are difficult questions. When they lead to ungodly envy, they result in the craving not only to grasp what others possess but also to make them pay for their pleasure and our deprivation. When they lead to ungodly jealousy, they result in clutching those who might walk away from us and threatening to harm them if they don't stay. At the core of jealousy and envy is a desperate desire to limit loss and guarantee satisfaction.

What is our hope when ungodly desire plants its bitter seeds deep in our souls? Jealousy and envy can be melted only in light of our astonishment at the passion of God's jealousy.

9

Divine Desire: The Jealous Love of God

It was four years after their breakup, but I (Tremper) could tell from Nan's eyes that she was still coping with the loss. I was at the door greeting people, having preached on Nahum 1, which begins: "The LORD is a jealous and avenging God; the LORD takes vengeance and is filled with wrath." She drew me aside and whispered, "I thought what I was feeling was so wrong. Now I realize that if I hadn't repressed my jealousy, maybe my family would be intact."

"What do you mean, Nan?" I asked her.

"I was taught from childhood that jealousy was just plain wrong. It was petty and selfish to be suspicious. So when I felt that way toward Mike, as he spent more and more time with Jessica, I just denied it. I shoved it away from me like the disgusting trash I thought it was."

Nan had divorced Mike four years ago, when she discovered that he had been sexually involved with her best friend, Jessica, for the previous two years. Nan didn't play tennis, and Mike enjoyed it so much that she didn't blink an eye when he asked her if she would mind if he played mixed doubles with Jessica at the country club. But their practice sessions were more than they were supposed to be.

"Now I see from the Bible that jealousy is not inherently bad. It can be, but not necessarily. God is jealous of His people, and He was right because the people were hurt by flirting with idols. God was protecting them from harm. I was jealous of Mike, but I kept pushing the feeling away in spite of the evidence. I was afraid of the struggle, but our relationship was worth it. I feel bad that I didn't lovingly confront him when I knew what was going on."

We're often afraid to acknowledge our intense desires of ambition, envy, and jealousy because we're afraid that we'll set ourselves up for disappointment. And further, some of us believe that we deserve nothing. Among religious people, this feeling of unworthiness is sometimes combined with a sense of guilt. Christians often take the attitude that they should be happy to be alive and have the promise of eternal life, and they are not worthy of what little they do have.

Our only desire should be Jesus, we tell ourselves. And indeed, Asaph, after struggling with envy, concluded, "Earth has nothing I desire besides you" (Psalm 73:25). But no matter how hard we try, intense desire still creeps into our lives, and we don't know what to do about it except to flagellate ourselves or deny the reality of our emotions. We comfort ourselves by saying, "It's not how we feel that's important; it's how we act."

But to turn away from intense desires is to miss the truth that ambition, envy, and jealousy can have a redemptive dimension.

DIVINE AND HUMAN JEALOUSY

Our God Is a Jealous God

At first glance, the language of Exodus 34:14 seems shocking: "Do not worship any other god, for the LORD, whose name is Jealous, is a jealous God."

God has many names in the Old Testament: Yahweh (the LORD), El Shaddai, the God of the fathers, the LORD of hosts. They all describe His character. The exact import of many of the names occasion vigorous debate among scholars. The name God receives in Exodus 34:14, however, is crystal clear. He is Jealous. Moses is thus affirming that jealousy is a divine trait.

Of whom is God jealous? Read long enough in the Old Testament and you'll know that He is jealous of idols, whose worship seduced Israel. God desires to protect His people when they cozy up to foreign gods. He yearns for intimate relationship and cannot stand it when someone or something else gets in the way, especially something as powerful and destructive as idolatry.

Moses calls God jealous in the context of presenting the Israelites with a brand-new set of the tablets engraved with the Ten Commandments. The first set had been smashed when Moses came down from Mount Sinai to find the Israelites worshiping a golden calf. God was furious, and in a jealous rage He called on the Levites to kill a number of the traitorous Israelites.

The Bible does not mince words. If God finds His wife, Israel, in bed with another god, He will kill them both. This message comes across loud and clear in Ezekiel 16, one of the most sexually graphic passages in the Bible. In vivid sexual imagery He recounts the history of His relationship with Israel. Israel's (geographic) mother and father had exposed their child at birth—throwing out the baby like so much garbage. This practice was the ancient equivalent to abortion—instead of killing the baby in the womb they waited until the child was born and then turned her over to the elements.

God saw the threatened child in the wilderness, took her in, cared for her, nurtured her. As the baby girl grew, she became beautiful. When the beautiful girl turned into a lovely woman, God says that He "spread the corner of my garment over you and covered your naked body" (16:8). This is the language of marriage and love-making. God, in essence, married Israel.

God then enhanced Israel's beauty so that she became well known throughout the entire world. But Israel shamelessly flaunted her body before other gods, even giving away the presents she had received from God to her idol-lovers.

Not surprisingly, God is jealous of His wife Israel. He will strip her naked in front of all her lovers and then take revenge against her by letting the lovers destroy her. This is the result of God's "jealous anger" (Ezekiel 16:38). The language is strong here, but it is found elsewhere as well (see, for instance, Ezekiel 23 and Hosea 1–3). The point is that God is legitimately jealous. We must not try to sanitize God's jealousy. As we see it at work in the Old Testament, it is an angry, resentful jealousy. People die in the face of it. God desires possession of what is His by right. His jealousy is as much a part of His nature as His love, compassion, and mercy.

To fathom the significance of this strong language, we must understand the basis for divine jealousy, which will set it apart from even justifiable human jealousy. Although human jealousy rarely reflects divine jealousy, they are similar; but they are never identical. God protects what He owns. He owns everything and everyone, including us, because He created us and sustains us.

Marriage is a mirror that reflects divine-human intimacy, but although this reflection is genuine, it is dim. We protect; we do not possess. One human being does not own another. The protection is based on the mutual marriage commitment.

Depending on the object of our protective desire and the means we use to express it, jealousy can be a righteous passion. If someone threatens the divine-human or marriage relationship, a resentful desire to shield the relationship is not only legitimate but honored. God sets a pattern for threatened spouses: an angry but dignified desire to repel the rival.

Envy is another matter, however. The Bible never prizes or condones a resentful desire to possess something or someone. Throughout Scripture, we are warned not to envy and taught that envy is an ugly human emotion. Indeed, it was envy that motivated the Judaean authorities to hand Jesus over to the Romans for execution.[1]

Envy is thus always wrong. As Asaph affirms in Psalm 73, we are to find our ultimate peace and security, our sense of well-being and esteem, in God alone. God reveals Himself as jealous, never as envious.

We should not be surprised that Jesus also reflects this divine characteristic. He was jealous of God's holy nature. When He saw it violated, He reacted violently. When He entered the Temple courts and saw sleazy businessmen using that holy area for their own profit, He drove them out with a whip. John understood that Jesus was displaying the jealousy expressed by David in Psalm 69:9—"Zeal [better translated jealousy] for your house consumes me." (See also John 2:17.)

Human Jealousy

Jealousy is a divine trait. But it can also be a legitimate human emotion. The Bible does not leave us in the dark here. Scripture clearly indicates that in some instances jealousy is more than appropriate: It is the only virtuous reaction to real threats to marriage.

Nan came to realize this truth. When she felt jealous of the time Mike spent with Jessica, she felt guilty. And that's exactly what Mike and Jessica wanted her to feel, because it enabled them to play on that guilt to carve out time to spend time together. Nan later realized that just as jealousy is a divine response to idolatry, so it can be a divinely instilled response to marital threats.

Why is jealousy appropriate in these two relationships, but not in other relationships? The answer is that the divine-human and the husband-wife relationships are the only two absolutely exclusive relationships. In no other relationship is there an element of exclusion of others.

JEALOUSY: PROTECTION OF AN EXCLUSIVE RELATIONSHIP

God will not tolerate His people having any other gods except Him, nor should a husband or wife tolerate any romantic or sexual rivals to their marriage relationship. Neither should a spouse accept the worship of false gods such as money, career, power, and position. All objects of addiction—whether alcohol, food, sex, work, or perfectionism—constitute idolatrous worship of a false god. Jealousy is an indicator that a greater love exists for a false god than for the path of life. A spouse ought to be jealous of any person or thing that saps passion for God and each other.

This is why biblical writers draw such a close connection between these two relationships, often teaching us about our relationship with God through marriage and vice versa. This connection is drawn not only in the Old Testament, of course, but also in the New, most notably in Ephesians 5:22-33, where we learn that husbands are to love their wives just as Christ loves the church.

Jealousy, therefore, is a legitimate emotion that God has given us in order to guard the important marriage relationship and keep the family intact. The love shared by a married couple is qualitatively different than any other kind of love in its exclusivity. No other love demands this unique commitment.

We should be careful how we understand this truth. Our love for our children is strong, but not exclusive to any one of them. I (Tremper) may—indeed must—love all three of my boys in special ways because each has different personalities and needs. It takes a wise parent to know which child is loved more by spending time with him and which is loved by providing space to mature. But it would be wrong for me to love only one of my three sons. It would be equally wrong of my children to begrudge the love that I show to the others.

A different ethic is at work in the marriage relationship. It would be wrong to share my wife sexually or tolerate her romantic intimacy with anyone else. Although it is necessary to grant the benefit of the doubt to a spouse on the principle that "love always trusts," it degrades the commitment of marriage to ignore obvious breaches of relationship.

This emotion is not based on a crude concept of marriage as possession. No one owns anyone else. But marriage is a mutual commitment to share life with a level of intimacy that is only possible between two—not three or four or more—people. A marriage must arouse and touch the desire for exclusivity. No one on the face of the earth is called to enter the soul of my wife as I am. No one is privileged to be a companion who knows, shares, and delights in the deepest parts of her soul as I do. And if I fail, then no other can succor the wound in comparison to my repentance.

This is not to imply that others, both male and female, are not to play a rich role in nurturing and enjoying my spouse. Frankly, to the degree that I love her well, she will be free to enter into various relationships with depth and passion. But all other connections with others will only invigorate a deeper desire for an exclusivity of physical and personal intimacy that can be touched nowhere else as it can in the marriage relationship.

Jealousy is the energy that drives the protection of that relationship. It is a relationship freely entered into, just as is our relationship with God. The fidelity of our relationship with God protects us from idols that will lure us away from Him and ultimately destroy us. But there is a difference between divine and human jealousy, and we must never lose sight of it. God has the right to possess and protect. We do not possess our spouse, but we do have the privilege of protection.

In certain situations in which loyalty to one another is compromised, jealousy is not an ugly suspicion that shows weakness, but a virtue that has a noble purpose: the preservation of an exclusive relationship. In these situations, to act on jealous feelings is to demonstrate courage in the face of danger. Indeed, it reflects God's own character as a God who protects His loved ones.

PROTECTIVE VERSUS ABUSIVE JEALOUSY

Under the apple tree I roused you;
there your mother conceived you,
there she who was in labor gave you birth.
Place me like a seal over your heart,
like a seal on your arm;
for love is as strong as death,
its jealousy unyielding as the grave.
It burns like blazing fire,
like a mighty flame.

Song of Songs 8:5-6

Jealousy is a strong emotion. The Song of Songs likens it to love and compares its power to that of fire. Fire can purify as well as destroy. Jealousy, which is God's signal to protect marriage, can be used to preserve or to destroy what is beautiful. No magic formulas can help here. It takes wisdom, strength, and tenderness to know when jealousy is redemptive and when it is destructive.

In order to evaluate the difference between protective and destructive jealousy, we must know our history as well as the current circumstances that have provoked the jealousy.

If there is a long history of jealousy in close relationships, it is likely that a deep strain of insecurity laced with vengeance is at play. This bitter root must be plucked before jealousy can be transformed from a true desire to protect the other into a demand to possess the other.

Current circumstances must be carefully assessed as well. Is there a pattern of distance? Is there repeated deceit? Even more, is there an unwillingness to face honestly and humbly the signals of idolatrous, or potentially idolatrous, patterns? A defensive response is always a violation of relationship, and therefore an indication that jealousy is appropriate. A willingness to interact, to hear, to argue, to feel the other person's point of view is usually an indication that jealousy is unwarranted.

Ungodly jealousy so often devolves into self-protection and pettiness that many people would just as soon blacken the emotion altogether. But biblical jealousy is never abusive. Although it might confront, it never harms or destroys.

THE LONGING FOR EXCLUSIVITY

Every person longs for exclusivity—a relationship that is single, special, unlike any other relationship on the face of the earth. Jealousy reflects a heart that not only faithfully protects, but exclusively desires. Who will surround me? Protect me against all others? Passionately pursue me alone, rather than any other?

We live a great deal of our lives unprotected, misunderstood, and lonely. Even in the best relationships, individuals are still left hungry for someone to comprehend their world and enter their struggle—to embrace them with a passion that seizes them and melts them into a union that will never be broken.

Obviously, this is not possible. No one will be faithful enough to lose all self-interest, to know and protect me against all harm. We all stray from intimacy and violate faithfulness. No one will be so aroused and delighted in me that she will neither see nor want any other. Even if it were possible, death itself ends all great loves. Our innate desire, again, seems to leave us feeling exposed and foolish.

Tragically, many marriages are either suffused with jealousy, destroying trust and passion, or deficient in jealousy, exposing the marriage as a functional union lacking depth and passion. We long to be protected and pursued. At its best, jealousy offers both. Human jealousy, though mired in sin, nevertheless reflects something of the jealous heart of God. And it is a glimpse of His jealous heart that allows us to be seized with desire to be loved exclusively without feeling foolish.

A PERFECTLY JEALOUS LOVER

God is a passionate paramour who spreads His blanket for love. He allures His bride into the desert for love. Jesus reveals Himself as our Bridegroom who will receive us in heaven at the marriage celebration.[2] God is our Spouse; we are His lover. And as our betrothed, He guards us jealously against any suitor who would tempt us away from our intimacy with Him.

No picture of God's faithfully protective, passionately exclusive love is clearer than the one revealed in how He addresses us. His special name for us reveals the passion of His heart.

Affectionate nicknames may be embarrassing, but we love them because they indicate endearment and privilege. Usually, no one else calls us by a special name but a family member, close friend, or lover. If the name is used by another, it can feel like a violation because it intrudes upon a special intimacy not open for sharing with outsiders.

What is God's name for us? He hints at it, but refuses to tell us:

> Whoever has ears, let them hear what the Spirit says to the churches. To the one who is victorious, I will give some of the hidden manna. I will also give that person a white stone with a new name written on it, known only to the one who receives it.
> *Revelation 2:17*

Heaven will hold a private encounter with God. At some point, we will taste pleasure beyond words. We will also receive a stone, pure and perfect, and on it will be a name. Our name will be known to no other—no person, no angel, no other being—but God.

When we hear that name, we will know that no other but God Himself has beckoned to us. We will know a level of intimacy and exclusivity that cannot be reckoned in any earthly experience of private, personal intimacy. His heart will be ours, and we will be wed to Him. Through that unique, exclusive name, there will be an intimacy that God will share with no other. His jealous love will possess us, protect us, and pursue us for eternity. And we will succumb to His pursuit in worship. Union will be undivided and sublime.

No wonder God hurts when we turn from Him to embrace the vile arms of another lover. No words can describe either the horror of that adultery or the depth of His anguish. To think we daily hold intimacy with Him in contempt, and look longingly at the pleasure that an idol can offer, staggers the imagination. How could it be that I shove my way past a six-course gourmet meal to throw myself on the carrion of a recent roadkill?

This adulterous rejection of divine intimacy incenses God: It provokes profound jealousy. Even more, it draws forth in God deep anguish. When we offer our exclusive devotion to another, jealousy torments His heart. His grief is revealed in this reflection on His rebellious child:

"Is not Ephraim my dear son,
    the child in whom I delight?
Though I often speak against him,
    I still remember him.
Therefore my heart yearns for him;
    I have great compassion for him,"
        declares the LORD.
Jeremiah 31:20

God's yearning is full of desire and pain. When He sees us violating love, He is moved to anger, jealousy, and torment. His pain can be heard in the Lord's cry, "Jerusalem, Jerusalem, you who kill the prophets and stone those sent to you, how often I have longed to gather your children together, as a hen gathers her chicks under her wings, and you were not willing" (Luke 13:34).

It is God's jealous love that both unnerves us and draws us to Him. His relentless pursuit, His fierce hatred of any rival, and His incomprehensible willingness to anguish on our behalf captures our heart for His love. His jealousy is our shield; it is our promise of eternal protection and passionate exclusivity. It is our confidence that the divine Lover will win His bride.

10

Abandonment and Despair:
The Loss of Hope

Thanksgiving day. What did she have to give thanks for? It was the fourth year in a row that she could not get out of bed to go to the table for the meal. It had to be brought to her.

Ninety-four Thanksgiving days, Melba thought to herself. *Eight in this wretched nursing home, four unable to walk to the table.*

She had nothing and nobody left in the world. Her husband had died thirty-five years before. Worked himself to death, worrying about making ends meet. She'd had no desire to get married again. Too old, she had thought at the time, and she still had her daughter and grandkids. Her daughter died last year at age seventy-three, a widow herself.

Why did Melba have to live to be so old and see her own child die? She wished with all her heart that she were already dead, as all her friends were. The memories of them wandered through her mind. Each face haunted her; each reminded her of the endless loss of life, friendship, and meaning. She was so tired. She wanted to quit, to turn her eyes away from the sorrow of life. *No one would care if I lived or died*, she thought as the tears rolled down her wrinkled cheeks.

DESPAIR: THE PASSIVE COUSIN OF JEALOUSY

Despair is the passive cousin of jealousy. Both are triggered by abandonment, which leads to loss of hope and loneliness. But while jealousy fights against loss, despair turns and runs. It is a refusal to struggle, deadening our hearts to the hope that we will be rescued, redeemed, and happy.

As with other emotions, the manifestations of despair spread across a spectrum of intensity: regret . . . sadness . . . depression . . . despair. Particular forms of loss of relationship are called grief or bereavement.

Regret describes a slight disappointment over loss. I (Tremper) remember hating piano lessons when I was young. The tunes were boring and my piano teacher was ancient. I much preferred being outside playing baseball. I finally convinced my long-suffering mother to cancel my lessons. With joy, I greeted my newfound freedom from practice and lessons. A few years later, the same pattern repeated itself with the guitar. Now, as I am moved by a piano concerto by Brahms or a guitar solo by Jimi Hendrix or Slash, I feel the loss of developing my musical ability. It is a slight loss, though, since I realize that life is full of give and take, and what little extra time I have is devoted to other enjoyments.

Sadness reaches deeper into our souls. An emptiness engendered by loss, sadness can make us cry in a way that regret cannot. It is a taste of the truth that the world is not all right, that creation is not what it was meant to be. But even though it is intense at times, sadness is also just a taste of loss. It comes and goes, usually attached to some specific cause.

My oldest son is getting closer and closer to college age. I (Tremper) hope that we will continue to be good friends even at a distance. But I also realize that once he leaves for college, my wife and I will see him less and less. As I anticipate his increasing absence from the home, it saddens me, even though this sense of loss is tempered by the unchanging fact that we are father and son and we care for each other.

Separations fueled by animosity or created by death are even deeper reaching and harder to overcome. But nonetheless, they do not necessarily lead to something life-absorbing, which is the defining trait of depression.

Sometimes we will flippantly say, "I'm depressed," when we really mean that we're sad. Depression is much more serious and incapacitating than sadness. We might characterize it as a continual state of mind rather than a temporary slowdown.

Depression can reveal itself in insomnia and an inability to concentrate on anything. Effort appears futile because it seems that nothing can really help or provide meaning. In the progression from regret to sadness to depression, the sense of loss is increasingly accompanied by a departure of hope. We are robbed of energy and the will to live. We cannot enjoy life.

The bottom floor of this progression is despair: the utter absence of any sense of hope, accompanied by a feeling of powerlessness. Despair leads to resignation and possibly to suicide. If you attended college in the sixties and seventies, you may recall the popularity of French existentialism. Some advocates of this philosophy suggested that suicide is the only logical response to the despair evoked by a meaningless world.

Despair looks at the world and notes its emptiness—the lack of true relational intimacy, the utter blackness of death. It concludes that life is not worth it. This is the core of all forms of destructive despair: abandonment, loss, the death of desire, and a subsequent refusal to hope.

OUR RESPONSE TO ABANDONMENT AND LOSS

Most of life is colored by loss. Some we can overcome with relative ease—the small pinpricks, paper cuts, bumps, and bruises that sting for a while and then go away. Others, such as dead dreams, lost loves, and broken promises, become lesions that no plastic surgery can camouflage. Loss through death or divorce, separation or betrayal, or any other form of abandonment strips the heart of any sense of constancy, security, and meaning.

A good friend recounted, in vivid terms, the moment he felt the wound of abandonment and loss. While he was cleaning the garage, listening to music, the phone rang. Annoyed, he went in to answer it.

"Hello," he said, hoping it would be a quick call.

"This is the suburban police. Are you the parent of Samantha Richards?"

Fear shuddered through his mind. "Yes, officer, what's wrong?"

"I'm afraid Samantha's been caught shoplifting with some friends. You must come to the station for questioning and to pick her up."

My friend tripped all over himself in a panic, changing clothes, finding keys—all the time questions coursing through his mind. *She's never been in trouble before. She's a normal kid—active in church and school, plenty of friends. There must be some mistake. What's going to happen to her?*

He hurried to the police station only to sit and wait in the lobby for an hour as the other parents were being questioned. Sadness gave way to depression. When he was finally called into the detective's office, the officer's opening words numbed his mind: "It was your daughter who actually stole the merchandise."

With Samantha released into her father's custody, they headed home. Both were devastated as they faced the next step: juvenile court. His depression began heading down into despair. What would happen in court? What would happen to his daughter?

As he drove in silence, he recalled the day of her birth. It had been a difficult birth, and the physicians had cautioned that she might not live. He had held her in his arms, gazing at her bright, wide-open stare. Then his thoughts flashed ahead to the engaging, precocious conversations they'd had when she was three. His mind continued to race through all the dreams he held for her, and he felt as if his life was crumbling along with hers.

She had betrayed him. She had abandoned her heritage and values and turned her back on his dreams for a stupid choice. One phone call, and he was plunged into feeling more hollow and alone than at any other moment in his life.

Though we may not be plunged into the despondency of despair, we all experience the loss of relationship and the subsequent loss of hope. Some may attempt to cover up their feelings by muttering pious platitudes—"Praise the Lord anyway"—or by shooing sadness away through immersion in the hectic busyness of life. But every once in a while, life catches us and brings us face to face with reality, and we feel what appears to be an inconsolable sadness.

For some, such feelings seem out of place in the Christian life— at least on the surface. Once again, though, the Bible cuts through our assumptions. The psalmist voices the cry of the soul as he struggles honestly with his emotions, which suggest to him that God does not care.

The Psalms are permeated with despair. When we read on in them, we notice that the psalmists consistently return to the Lord with joy and confidence. This might give us the impression that the psalmists' cry is simply a brief episode, setting up the praise at the end. But this is a misunderstanding, because what appears to us to be a quick transition from crying to rejoicing is actually the culmination of a long struggle.

Another impression we might form upon reading the Psalms is that only those who break out of despondency make the grade and get their psalms included in the Psalter. Psalm 88 disabuses us of that conclusion. The author, whom the title identifies as Heman the Ezrahite, laments:

> LORD, you are the God who saves me;
>> day and night I cry out to you.
> May my prayer come before you;
>> turn your ear to my cry.
>
> I am overwhelmed with troubles
>> and my life draws near to death.
> I am counted among those who go down to the pit;
>> I am like one without strength.
> I am set apart with the dead,
>> like the slain who lie in the grave,
> whom you remember no more,
>> who are cut off from your care.
>
> You have put me in the lowest pit,
>> in the darkest depths.
> Your wrath lies heavily on me;
>> you have overwhelmed me with all your waves.
> You have taken from me my closest friends
>> and have made me repulsive to them.
> I am confined and cannot escape;
>> my eyes are dim with grief.
>
> I call to you, LORD, every day;
>> I spread out my hands to you.
> Do you show your wonders to the dead?
>> Do their spirits rise up and praise you?

Is your love declared in the grave,
    your faithfulness in Destruction?
Are your wonders known in the place of darkness,
    or your righteous deeds in the land of oblivion?

But I cry to you for help, LORD;
    in the morning my prayer comes before you.
Why, LORD, do you reject me
    and hide your face from me?

From my youth I have suffered and been close to death;
    I have borne your terrors and am in despair.
Your wrath has swept over me;
    your terrors have destroyed me.
All day long they surround me like a flood;
    they have completely engulfed me.
You have taken from me friend and neighbor—
    darkness is my closest friend.

Psalm 88:1-18

This psalm is the blackest of all the laments in the Psalter. The composer's agonizing scream can be heard from beginning to end, because his pain has lasted from his youth until now. The only glimmer of hope in the entire psalm is the fact that the psalmist bothers to pray at all, referring to God as the one "who saves me."

The final line, however, indicates that the psalmist is on the edge of emotional obliteration. Friends have abandoned him, and he blames God for this. Worse yet, however, in his suffering God does not draw close to him, but rather is painfully absent. His most intimate companion is the darkness of oblivion. Only in the shadows of sleep or deep repression does he find relief. The natural corollary is that death, the ultimate darkness, is the only solution.

The psalmist feels assaulted in life on many different levels. He feels completely isolated, set apart from others (verse 5). He is overwhelmed with troubles, likening his life to standing up to his neck in water as the waves roll over him, making it impossible for him to catch his breath (verse 7). He is not isolated by chance; he is despised by other people, particularly those who used to be his friends (verse 8). Most horrifying of all, as he approaches the grave he feels utterly abandoned by God (verse 14)—not just ignored by Him, but rejected.

Psalm 88 is a powerful testimony to the experience of teetering on the edge of utter despair. The slightest puff of wind will push him into the blackness of death, a fate that both frightens and entices him. His greatest comfort is not finding comfort in hope, but burrowing deeper into darkness.

The Refusal to Hope

When life is full of problems or when we're filled with anger or fear toward those who assault us, hope allows us to go on with living. It gives us some sense that things are going to get better. Life will improve, and the problems besieging us will reach some stage of resolution. Once the pain is over, we will again enjoy life.

Hope is the anticipation that desires in the present will be satisfied in the near future. Gabriel Marcel calls hope a "memory of the future." I may be disappointed with the relationships in my life, but hope sustains me by holding out the promise of something new and positive on the road ahead.

In many ways, hope is intangible—it is a concept or a feeling. But on a practical level, it is tangible: in a sense, people incarnate hope. As a product of relationship, hope comes to us in human form. In contrast, loneliness is the breeding ground for despair.

Often, our hope is simply naive. It simply trusts that things will soon work out as we desire. This is actually magical desire. Hope centered in a person puts our future in their hands, so that we trust them to accomplish what we cannot do ourselves. Inevitably, naive and human-centered hope leads to profound disillusionment. And when hope is shattered, it is usually too painful to hope again.

"Hope deferred makes the heart sick, but a longing fulfilled is a tree of life," declares the writer of Proverbs (13:12). We desire fulfillment, but disappointment robs us of stability, sending us reeling under the sickness of despair. Over time, the often-repeated cycle of desire aroused, hope disappointed, and soul deadened through despair leads to a hatred of desire.

This cycle is traveled by many who have experienced deferred hope. It is perhaps seen most clearly in the lives of those who have experienced profound betrayal.

I (Dan) worked with a woman who had been sexually abused by her brother over a period of eight years. Not only did he abuse her, he sold her to other boys in the neighborhood. Every time her mother left the older brother in charge at home, Maria would beg her mother to take her along. Maria would often become so ill that she would hyperventilate and collapse. Her mother would laugh at her daughter's protestations and accuse her of theatrical manipulation.

The abuse stopped only after the brother was killed in a car accident. After he died, Maria felt alive and free. She allowed herself to hope that maybe her mother might care for her, as she had cared for her son. Maria worked hard to help her mother cope with the loss, serving the family for years before she finally told her mother about the abuse.

When Maria finally shared with her mother about her years of torment, her mother responded, "If you ever repeat a lie like that about your brother, I will never again speak to you or call you my daughter."

Through all the years of abuse, Maria had believed that her mother did not know; if she had known, certainly she would have rescued her daughter. Now, her mother's refusal to hear, to believe—even more, the threat of being severed from the family—killed Maria's fragile hope of being loved by her mother.

For nearly a decade after that interaction, Maria lived in the nether world of despair. She eventually married, ran a business, and conducted herself well in church and social activities. But she was a zombie—one of the waking dead who live with robotic precision but exist without desire and passion.

It is far easier to snuff out desire with the shroud of despair than to live with the ache of deferred desire.

The Flight from Desire

Maria illustrates what is at the heart of despair—a flight from desire. Desire so often proves fruitless. Disappointment has answered hope so many times that it seems utterly absurd to continue to hunger or yearn for anything any longer. To hope is to become vulnerable to more pain. The best solution, therefore, seems to be to completely shut down, become robot-like, and expect absolutely nothing out of life.

At first, this thought may seem harsh. A person in despair does need encouragement and assistance. But rarely will encouragement or help lift a person out of the slough of despondency. Something else must occur—facing honestly the loss and the terror that is even more painful than the despair. In this sense, despair is like a blanket that can be pulled over the head to escape the first rays of dawn and the sound of the alarm clock. It is the subterfuge of fleeing from the disappointment of deferred desire that torments the heart with a sickness unto death.

LONELINESS: THE WITHDRAWAL OF INTIMACY

Inevitably, a loss of hope leads to loneliness: the absence or loss of relationship. Loneliness is isolation from those who mean the most to us.

This isolation is not necessarily physical. Tim Keller, pastor of Redeemer Church in Manhattan, has rightly stated that married people are often the most lonely people around. Just because you are in the same house with someone or even sleep in the same bed does not automatically mean that you are in an intimate relationship with that person. What makes the loneliness of marriage so painful is the irony: God created the institution so that people would not feel lonely.

The author of the book of Ecclesiastes, who keenly recognized the evil and meaninglessness of life in this world, had very little positive to say about the world except to tip his hat to relationship:

> Two are better than one,
>> because they have a good return for their labor:
> If either of them falls down,
>> one can help the other up.
> But pity anyone who falls
>> and has no one to help them up.
> Also, if two lie down together, they will keep warm.
>> But how can one keep warm alone?
> Though one may be overpowered,
>> two can defend themselves.
> A cord of three strands is not quickly broken.
> *Ecclesiastes 4:9-12*

Without human relationship to provide us with encouragement and hope, the world seems dangerous, cold, and profitless—in a word, meaningless. This perception leads to deeper, chronic despair when we respond to abandonment by running from desire and escaping into lonely isolation.

WHEN HOPE IS LOST

Few experience the numbness of despair for long, but we have all been on the road of regret, sadness, and even depression that leads to the blackness of despondency. Before shoving the memory of these destructive emotions away from us, let's pause and ask what they tell us about the world and about ourselves.

Despair looks at the world and says, "Meaningless! Meaningless! . . . Everything is meaningless!" (Ecclesiastes 1:2). In this response, despair rightly describes conditions as they are. The world is not a warm, fuzzy place full of hope and cheer. It is a dark, dangerous realm against which we are totally defenseless.

Despair looks at the world and says, "I am alone. No one can help me. No one cares about me." Worse still, people stand against me. They not only avoid helping me; they try to make my life even more miserable than it is.

Despair looks at the world and says, "I have no hope. Things are not going to get better." They can't get worse, but they will constantly stay at the same low. Any indication that they might get better is an illusion. Therefore, I must not allow myself to hope again, because I will only be bitterly disappointed.

We live in a sinful world in which not all expectations are met, not all relationships succeed, and not all hopes come true. This description of life conforms to what the Bible tells us in the first three chapters of the book of Genesis. God created the world good and designed relationships to be fulfilling. But human evil was introduced into life's experiences, resulting in alienation in human relationships. This biblical account profoundly describes human experience as we know it: created good, yet frequently experienced as evil and lonely.

However, the Bible does not end with Genesis 3. Hundreds of chapters follow, continuing the story of God's involvement with a sinful, fallen world. The rest of the Bible addresses the problems raised in the first three chapters. Specifically, Genesis 4 and following invite us to question whether despair, although it rightly understands the human condition, is the final answer.

Psalm 88, and many other grief psalms as well, are models to us of frank, brutally honest conversation with God. The conversation gets messy at times; but then, life is messy. The psalmist convicts us of our tendency to sweep all of our ugly emotions toward God and ourselves under the rug. By his example, the psalmist invites us to open ourselves up to the Lord. We yearn to unburden ourselves to Him. The good news of the Psalms is, we can!

Despair is an absence of hope—a loss of desire in the face of disappointment in relationship. Oddly, however, this difficult emotion can open the heart to grasp something about a hope that transcends mere human relationship. Despair can open the heart to taste hope in God.

11

Redemptive Despair: The Restoration of Hope

Ungodly despair is a flight from desire; it is a refusal to embrace loss as a deepening of the hollowness that makes more room for God. Despair refuses to dream, to hope, and to move with courage toward what we will one day become. It flees to an illusory safe harbor where, isolated, it holds onto whatever pleasure comes from the fantasy of nonexistence.

This is why suicide, the choice of nonexistence, is often preferred to hope: It allows those in despair to shield their hearts from the agony of becoming. Ungodly despair refuses to walk through the valley of the shadow of death; it refuses to agonize any longer with the pangs of uncertainty, loss, and the irrepressible desire for redemption.

Godly despair is the collapse of self-will; it is the surrender to a reality of becoming that we are powerless to consummate but in which we are granted an opportunity to play a part. Instead of a suicide note that puts a stop to the loss, it is a howling prayer that sees no explanation for our pain but reflexively knows something beyond an answer is what we desire. Although ungodly despair demands an answer for the loss, it would refuse to accept an answer even if it were hand-delivered by God. Godly despair cries out for perspective but allows the hollowness of loss to move the heart to seek God.

The Bible rips off the skin of pretense and reveals the disease within. The courage of the psalmists exposes the illusion of a blissful world. The hope of the psalmists compels us to direct our despair to God. Psalm 77 begins our journey.

PSALM 77:1-9—A MIDNIGHT STRUGGLE

Perhaps no more intense expression of anxiety and fear may be found in the Bible than in these opening verses of Psalm 77:

> I cried out to God for help;
> > I cried out to God to hear me.
> When I was in distress, I sought the Lord;
> > at night I stretched out untiring hands,
> > and I would not be comforted.
>
> *Psalm 77:1-2*

The psalmist does not name the specific trouble that induced his depression, but it was so intense that he could not sleep at night. Rather than trying to fight off his troubled thoughts and seek the temporary forgetfulness of sleep, he spent his time praying. He turned toward his struggle instead of away from it, laying out his torment before God:

> I remembered you, God, and I groaned;
> > I meditated, and my spirit grew faint.

You kept my eyes from closing;
> I was too troubled to speak.
I thought about the former days,
> the years of long ago;
I remembered my songs in the night.
> My heart meditated and my spirit asked:
"Will the Lord reject forever?
> Will he never show his favor again?
Has his unfailing love vanished forever?
> Has his promise failed for all time?
Has God forgotten to be merciful?
> Has he in anger withheld his compassion?"

Psalm 77:3-9

First, he goes straight to God. But instead of strength and joy, he experiences a deeper and more sickening depression. As he remembers God, he groans: It is God who keeps him from sleeping! It is God who torments him! It is God who has abandoned him and left him to twist and turn in agony in bed at night!

The psalmist is engaged in a deep struggle with God over his fears and depression. He demands an accounting from God. In his anxiety, he throws God's promises back in His divine face.

Long ago, God had promised to be with His people in a covenant relationship. That meant He would protect them and watch over them. He had promised to show them "favor," "unfailing love," to be "merciful," and keep His "promise." The psalmist confronts God here and demands to know whether He is a liar. In the midst of his pain, he looks at his situation and wonders if God has reneged on His promises to him.

We are too quick to explain away this kind of language. Most of us would be scared to death to talk to God this way. But what do we do instead? We repress our strong emotions, and too quickly and unreflectively "turn it over to God." If we are honest with our-selves, however, we don't really put it in God's hands—we bottle it up within ourselves. The problem continues to exist, and our fear festers and grows inside of us, alienating us not only from our true emotions but also from God.

The irony of faith is that it is not a quiet submission to the fates. It asks, and it shouts; it is a cry that is heard in heaven. Faith does not affect pious language, nor does it presume that honest struggle will be smashed in a fit of divine pique. The irony of questioning God is that it honors Him: It turns our hearts away from ungodly despair toward a passionate desire to comprehend Him.

PSALM 77:10-20—A DIVINE BULWARK AGAINST DEPRESSION

As the psalmist recounts his midnight battle against his fears and against God, he experiences a remarkable change. This inversion takes him from the pit of his own private hell to the heights of joy. He leaves us in no doubt about the reason for his change of mind:

> Then I thought, "To this I will appeal:
>   the years when the Most High stretched out his right hand.
> I will remember the deeds of the LORD;
>   yes, I will remember your miracles of long ago.
> I will consider all your works
>   and meditate on all your mighty deeds."
> *Psalm 77:10-12*

His thoughts turn from his troubles toward God, specifically to God's past acts of deliverance. In particular, the psalmist remembers what is perhaps the greatest salvation event in the Old Testament, the Exodus from Egypt:

The waters saw you, God,
> the waters saw you and writhed;
> the very depths were convulsed.

The clouds poured down water,
> the heavens resounded with thunder;
> your arrows flashed back and forth.

Your thunder was heard in the whirlwind,
> your lightning lit up the world;
> the earth trembled and quaked.

Your path led through the sea,
> your way through the mighty waters,
> though your footprints were not seen.

You led your people like a flock
> by the hand of Moses and Aaron.

Psalm 77:16-20

By the time this psalm was composed, the Exodus was already an event of the far-distant past. It was ancient history to the psalmist, just as it is to us. But notice how it helps him to remember this event. He puts himself back in the time of the deliverance from Egypt, recognizing that the danger confronting the Israelites was far more frightening than his own problems. They had their backs up against an impassable sea as the Egyptian army bore down on them. Talk about helpless! They were sitting ducks before the anger of a shamed Pharaoh. God, however, not only delivered the Israelites but also destroyed the Egyptians through the act of splitting the sea and then closing it again.

The psalmist's memory of the Exodus becomes a bulwark against his present troubles. If God could deliver His people from such dire troubles and deep fears in the past, He can certainly handle any present problems.

The Significance of Memory

Memory plays a crucial role in the Bible. It has an important role to play in faith. We tend to think of memory as a purely mental act, referring merely to the ability to recall something to mind. In the Bible, however, it means far more. It is not just thought; it includes imagination. It is the borrowing of "history" as a picture of our current story.

For instance, when the psalmist calls on God to remember His people (74:2), he asks God to do more than think about Israel; he calls on God to save them. He invites God to save now as He did in the past. Similarly, when the psalmist says he remembers "the deeds of the LORD" (77:11), he has in mind more than the mere fact that he can recite the events surrounding the Exodus. It means that he has and is experiencing the Exodus in his own life at that very moment!

Memory is not mere nostalgia. It is a creative borrowing of the past as a template of what we hope for the present. To remember the past is to reshape the present with desire and hope.

Many of us can point to events in our personal past that demonstrate how God can save us from trouble. In this sense we, too, have participated in the Exodus. The event may have been something quite small on a cosmic scale but huge on a personal level—a check that arrived at a time when we were experiencing severe financial difficulties; the gift of a new friend during a period of loneliness; divine intervention in the form of timely healing from disease or injury.

God has likely demonstrated both His willingness and His ability to help you in difficult times in the past. By remembering these gracious acts, your confidence in God will be strengthened in the present. The psalmist attests to this. He now remembers the past, and this allows him to stop tossing and turning with midnight anxiety and exclaim:

Your ways, God, are holy.
What god is as great as our God?

You are the God who performs miracles;
>   you display your power among the peoples.
With your mighty arm you redeemed your people,
>   the descendants of Jacob and Joseph.

Psalm 77:13-15

The psalmist, through his memory—and thus his experience—of who God is and what He has done, has a change of heart. He moves from depression to affirmation of the Lord.

REDEMPTIVE ABANDONMENT

Left alone in a world full of trouble—what could be worse? But God is cunning; He knows how to get our attention. Rather than let us wallow in the mediocrity of complacency, He lets us experience what it would be like to live without Him. He abandons us in order to shatter our illusions and then to lead us to a deeper relationship with Him. We see this pattern again and again in Scripture, both on a corporate and an individual level.

God put up with a tremendous amount of disregard, even abuse, from the Israelites through their history. Over and over He demonstrated to them that He was a patient God. But the Israelites settled into a contented indifference toward God. Yes, they believed He existed. They also believed that He would protect them whether or not they worshiped Him or paid any attention to Him. After all, He lived in Jerusalem. Surely He would not allow His own house, the Temple, to be touched by foreign armies.

This attitude was captured by the prophet Jeremiah, who warned the people to change their ways and quit sitting around assuring themselves: "Do not trust in deceptive words and say, 'This is the temple of the LORD, the temple of the LORD, the temple of the LORD!'" (Jeremiah 7:4).

God knew that radical action was required in order to get the attention of His callused people. So He moved out of Jerusalem. Chapters 9–11 of Ezekiel chart God's departure from the innermost part of the Temple to the threshold (9:3); from there He mounted His heavenly chariot driven by angelic cherubim (11:18-22). The last place we see God is on mountains east of Jerusalem (11:23-24), heading toward Babylon.

The next time God appears, He is at the head of the Babylonian army (Jeremiah 21:3-7), which He used to bring judgment against Israel. But through judgment came salvation. Out of the rubble of exile came the restoration: a new, devoted Israel, ready to serve the Lord (see the books of Ezra and Nehemiah).

This pattern of redemptive abandonment can also be seen on an individual level in Psalm 30, a prayer of thanks to God for salvation from death. While thanking God, David remembers the danger he was in:

> When I felt secure, I said,
>   "I will never be shaken."
> LORD, when you favored me,
>   you made my royal mountain stand firm;
> but when you hid your face,
>   I was dismayed.
> *Psalm 30:6-7*

David remembers the complacency he felt, which resulted from the confidence he had in his own strength. Nothing could happen to him—he was too good, too strong, too competent, too powerful. But when God abandoned David by "hiding his face," God stripped away from David his illusion of self-confidence. Predictably, the result of this abandonment was loss of hope: depression.

But where did this depression drive David—to self-pity? No. It drove him into the arms of God:

> To you, LORD, I called;
>   to the Lord I cried for mercy:
> "What is gained if I am silenced,
>   if I go down to the pit?
> Will the dust praise you?
>   Will it proclaim your faithfulness?
> Hear, LORD, and be merciful to me;
>   LORD, be my help."
>
> *Psalm 30:8-10*

Once again, the pattern moves from complacency, to abandonment, to depression, to greater glory—from stagnant relationship, to loneliness, to intimate fellowship:

> You turned my wailing into dancing;
>   you removed my sackcloth and clothed me with joy,
> that my heart may sing your praises and not be silent.
>   LORD my God, I will praise you forever.
>
> *Psalm 30:11-12*

HEAVENLY HOPE

Hope has two goals, one earthly and the other heavenly. It is not that one is evil and the other good. They both can be good, but heavenly hope must envelop earthly hope in order to give it value.

Earthly, or horizontal, hope is the confident desire that things are going to get better in this life. My marriage will improve; my children will grow up to become productive believers in a fallen world.

Earthly hope is fragile, because decay and death are always around the corner. Just when things seem to be working well, something goes wrong. Just as my relationship with my wife becomes more intimate and fulfilling, I get a cut in pay at work. Just as I get my children through college, my doctor warns me about my risk of heart disease.

Heavenly hope is a vision of redemption in the midst of the decay. Its source is in God, and its focus is that we will become more and more like Him and that we will always be with Him. Heavenly hope transcends even death, because we know that death does not sever our relationship, nor can loss keep us from becoming like God.

Apart from heavenly hope, earthly hope has only one destination: inevitable disappointment. But heavenly hope provides the substance that allows us also to hope here on earth. God is at work in the circumstances of my life. When there are setbacks, I do not have to give in to complete despondency, because my ultimate hope is in God, who will never let me down.

The surprising truth is that God uses the emptiness that induces depression to drive us to Him. This in turn gives rise to greater joy, and to heavenly hope. We live in a world created beautiful but tainted by human sin. As we see the world for what it really is, we have a choice—despair or God.

Thankfully, despair is seasonal. It is God's severe mercy for a time, not a chronic condition of every moment of life. We are told there is a time for despair, but also for rejoicing. Heavenly hope does not preclude despair. But it assures us that although there may be crying in the night, there will rejoicing in the morning.

We can see this truth vividly portrayed in the Son of God.

THE REDEMPTIVE DESPAIR OF CHRIST

Jesus experienced the fallen world with sadness. He suffered when He was tempted. And He was tempted in every way, just as we are.[1]

How ironic is the scene at the grave of Lazarus (John 11:17-43). Jesus had arrived too late; His good friend had just died. When He was taken to Lazarus's resting place, the Son of God sobbed.

The irony is that Jesus' next act was to revive Lazarus from death—so why did He bother to cry? Why weep when He knew that He had the power to resurrect the dead?

Jesus knew that death was inevitable in a fallen world. He understood that, though Lazarus would live again, he would also die again. The Bible does not record the second death of Lazarus, but it surely happened. Jesus wept, perhaps, because He understood that death was real, that death severed relationships and dashed hopes.

But this was just a taste of what was to come for Jesus. He experienced the horror of despair at the climax and conclusion of His life. The last days of His life began with the triumphal entry into Jerusalem. Thousands of people greeted Him as their king as He entered the holy city, riding on a mule. This mode of entry was not a sign of lowliness, but an indication of royal power in the fulfillment of the prophecy in Zechariah 9:9.

This affirmation and affection was short-lived, however. As the religious and political authorities turned against Jesus, so the crowds deserted Him. As time wore on, even His close associates, the disciples, began to waver in their support—as we see in the reactions of the three disciples who were closest to Him: Peter, James, and John.

Jesus sought solitude in the garden of Gethsemane because He struggled with what He knew was ahead for Him. Here, Jesus teetered on the edge of despair. He said as much to the three when He asked them to keep watch: "My soul is overwhelmed with sorrow to the point of death" (Matthew 26:38). Luke tells us that Jesus, "being in anguish . . . prayed more earnestly, and his sweat was like drops of blood falling to the ground" (Luke 22:44).

Jesus bore the full weight of the curse, accomplishing His labor with the sweat of His brow to the point of sweating blood. He was in agony, and He came to His friends for communion. But He found His friends asleep—perhaps because they were exhausted with sorrow. This abandonment, during His time of real need, shocked Jesus. In essence, it was a betrayal of the highest order. And it happened again and again, three times all together. Nonetheless, Jesus refused to give in to despair. Each time He continued to ask them for what He desired: their help and support. The repeated sorrow did not cause Him to retreat into Himself. On the contrary, He worried more for them than for Himself.

But the betrayals continued and intensified as time progressed. Judas, one of the intimate twelve, turned Jesus in to the authorities. Peter, another close friend and disciple, denied ever knowing Him.

Jesus was alone in the world. No human being would be with Him to comfort Him, to aid Him as He faced the forces of evil in the world. But none of this even compares with what happened on the cross.

Jesus was nailed to the cross and then lifted up to twist and squirm in physical agony, trying to breathe, His hands and feet torn by the nails. Suddenly, His voice rent the air with the cry, "My God, my God, why have you forsaken me?"[2]

Not only had His human companions abandoned Him, but now God, His Father, had also deserted Him. At that moment, He experienced despair like no human being has ever experienced it. At that point, hopelessness achieved a new definition. How could there ever be hope for any human being if God the Father refused to relieve the agony of God the Son? If He refused to save His own Son, then what would He do with the rest of humanity—enemies and rebels? Death followed.

Note the origin of Jesus' cry from the cross—the Psalms. Jesus found His own emotions expressed by the cry of the psalmist, specifically Psalm 22. As Ridderbos explained, "This shows how deep his suffering was; it was the sum of all the pain and distress that had been cried out in the prophetic laments of the Old Testament as a model for and prefiguration of Jesus's suffering."[3] Psalm 22 in particular gave voice to His pain, and He fulfilled this psalm literally in more than one respect. His body and soul were torn apart (verse 14); His hands and feet were pierced (verse 16); and His garments were divided by casting lots (verse 18).

But Jesus' most intense suffering was not physical. It stemmed from His sense of complete abandonment by His Father. We must not think of Christ's suffering as a pretense, a fiction. His pain and distress were incomprehensible. God's abandonment and Jesus' consequent intense loneliness and despair were very real.

THE TRANSFORMATION OF SUFFERING

Beyond the atonement for sin, God had a purpose for Christ's embrace of the pain of the world. The despair of the cross not only gives us a model for embracing loss and the assurance that we are not alone in facing it, but, more importantly, it transforms all human suffering.

Suffering seems so pointless, meaningless. Rarely can we say honestly, without contrivance, "I see why God allowed this loss to occur." More often, we are at a loss to comprehend loss. It is a double sorrow—not only do we experience despair, but the despair makes no sense.

The cross cuts to the core of all suffering, all loss, all despair by invading it with the cry, "My God, my God." The cross paradoxically transforms all human sorrow from a horizontal loss to a vertical agony that compels us to ask God who He is. The Lord's cry will never allow us to see human suffering as merely accidental or incidental to life. All loss is bound to God.

Far more, Jesus' cry of despair also transforms all human suffering as a promise. It is a down payment on hope. Jesus suffered, and so will we. But He has been there before us; He waits for us at the end of our sorrow. He has been perfected and resurrected through suffering; so will we.

Nothing could be more astonishing than that Jesus, perfectly mature as the sinless man, became perfect and mature through suffering:

> But we do see Jesus, who was made lower than the angels for a little while, now crowned with glory and honor because he suffered death, so that by the grace of God he might taste death for everyone.
>
> In bringing many sons and daughters to glory, it was fitting that God, for whom and through whom everything exists, should make the pioneer of their salvation perfect through what he suffered.
> *Hebrews 2:9-10*

The cry of dereliction transforms all human tears into a prayer before God. Further, the cross transforms all human suffering from a meaningless waste to a condition for glory which He chose to pioneer as the firstfruits of what will one day be a harvest of our own glorification.

Therefore, I cannot sorrow over the loss of life, betrayal, and abandonment without anticipating the dawning day of utter redemption. I cannot weep without sensing that each tear is caught in the crevice of His wounds, mingled with His sorrow, and saved as a rare perfume to anoint His glory.

Neither am I free to sorrow and despair in isolation. I must sorrow, even despair, in communion with others who live with some awareness of the same cry of dereliction and the same hope of resurrection.

THE GLORY OF DESPAIR

Recently, I (Dan) was privileged to be one who spoke at the funeral of a dear friend's twelve-year-old son. I watched Alan and Sally greet people who came to say good-bye to Ben. As they embraced some, there was a flood of tears; with others, there was laughter— an oddly compelling laughter that borrowed hope from heaven. I was transfixed. I could not keep my eyes off them. They wept. They laughed. They knew something I long to know. Although I despise and fear the path on which they have learned it, I desperately want to know what they know, what brought forth streams of both sorrow and laughter.

Loss, sorrow, and despair compel us to seek out our friends, even when they slumber in denial. Our shared despair compels us to strain to hear the barely audible yet undeniable laughter of heaven. It is that sound that transforms despair into a gift of hope. It is a taste of the presence of God.

As we enter into the transformation of despair, at times our lives will be filled with great pleasure and joy. At other times, we will be overcome by a sadness that seems like death itself. If we are willing not to hide under despair, but to call forth to those who abandon us—even more, to call forth to the One who seems to have turned His face—we will discover the paradox of His presence in the midst of His absence. Or, more accurately said, we will find Him after we have given up making Him in our image. Despair exposes our emptiness and the futility of our idol-making. If our hearts hunger for Him, then despair is our ally, our friend, our guide, opening our hearts to the bright hope of seeing His face.

As we fathom the emptiness of despair, we gain a deeper understanding of Jesus' willingness to empty Himself of His glory and to sorrow alone on our behalf. Through our sadness, we learn something about the heart of our Lord. In this way, despair catapults us not into the dark abyss, but into the bright presence of God.

12

Unholy Contempt: Evil's Mockery

Nothing hurts quite like being mocked, taunted, or violated with contempt. Our childhoods reverberate with the memories of so-called harmless derision—the haunting laughter ringing on the playground after a failure to make it to the bathroom, the sneers in the gym shower when maturation came too slowly or too quickly.

A professional athlete recalled a day in fourth grade when he was the last boy chosen for a game of softball. He was overweight and awkward. He remembers the disdain in the eyes of those picked first, and the protests and scorn when he was finally selected. That day he swore an oath that drove him to work out daily, improve his speed, and intensify his aggression. He later became an all-star baseball player, drafted out of high school to play professional ball. He attributes his success to his determination never to be mocked again.

A woman who was humiliated by boys' taunts and harassments as

THE CRY OF THE SOUL

she was beginning to mature in adolescence gained national promi-
nence in the field of victims' rights.

A brilliant scientist who as a young man suffered repeated rejec-
tions when he asked girls out for a date chose to work in the isolation
of test tubes and arcane scientific formulas.

Perhaps more than any other force, contempt shapes our life
vows and commitments. No childhood chant could be more untrue:
"Sticks and stones may break my bones, but words will never hurt
me." Venomous words of contempt, mockery, and derision can crush
the soul and deaden the heart to the call of God.

Contempt is an assault against the glory God intends His children
to bear. It sears and stings, mirroring the mockery of evil. In fact, no
emotion is more often chosen by the evil one to assault the gospel
than contempt.

Why is contempt so powerful? Why is it so often the prime weapon
of the arrogant to control the weak?

THE POWER OF CONTEMPT

Some time ago, I (Dan) met with a man who was angry at the counsel I had offered his wife. Janet was sweet to the point of being syr-
upy. She had endured her husband's sixteen-hour work days, chronic
verbal abuse, and occasional purchases of pornography by burying
her head in the sand with unholy patience and emotional deadness.

Our work had exposed Janet's silent fury. She began to see how
often she sabotaged their sexual relationship and undermined his
relationship with their kids. She was hurt and vindictive, but through
a painful and redemptive process, she finally moved to love and
honor her husband. In the process, she made life more difficult for
him than he had ever experienced in twenty-two years of marriage.
Now he wanted to talk with me.

Our first talk was filled with adversarial tension. His words were full of anger: "I am not happy with what I see happening in Janet. Your work with her is ruining our marriage."

I did not respond to his angry attack. I did not attempt to explain myself or apologize for his pain. I was saddened. "Sir," I asked, "what do you want to accomplish in our time together?"

Furious that his angry assault had provoked neither fight nor flight, he shifted to the cold, calculating venom of contempt. Cocking his head and narrowing his eyes, he snarled: "Young man, I am here to expose you as an arrogant, destructive wolf in sheep's clothing. You will not get away with destroying my marriage."

Thus began one of my worst hours of counseling. Over the next hour I was subjected to taunt after taunt.

Prior to that encounter, I had been somewhat convinced that Janet was loving her husband well. But after that hour with him, having sustained countless piercing jabs of disdain and egged on by his mockery, I felt caught in a vortex of self-doubt, exhausted at swimming against the undertow and willing to blame Janet for the problems in the marriage. I also felt enraged—not merely angry, but incensed to the degree that I wanted to hurt someone or something.

The combination of self-doubt, exhaustion, and fury fulfilled what he said about me and seduced me to turn my back on what I knew to be true. Compromise seemed better than the prospect of facing his cold, venomous mockery. The effect of his contempt was to make me feel weak and deluded.

Contempt is a form of anger. Anger intimidates and controls, provoking us to battle or retreat. Contempt ups the ante, intensifying our fight or flight exponentially. In provoking us to retaliate with contempt or kill desire with numbing shame, it violates and destroys.

One reason for the extraordinary power of contempt is that it isolates us as unlovable, withering our hope for love.

Contempt Isolates and Withers

Because of all my enemies,
    I am the utter contempt of my neighbors
and an object of dread to my closest friends—
    those who see me on the street flee from me.
I am forgotten as though I were dead;
    I have become like broken pottery.
For I hear many whispering,
    "Terror on every side!"
They conspire against me
    and plot to take my life.

Psalm 31:11-13

I am like a desert owl,
    like an owl among the ruins.
I lie awake; I have become
    like a bird alone on a roof.
All day long my enemies taunt me;
    those who rail against me use my name as a curse.
For I eat ashes as my food
    and mingle my drink with tears
because of your great wrath,
    for you have taken me up and thrown me aside.
My days are like the evening shadow;
    I wither away like grass.

Psalm 102:6-11

Contempt is a poison that paralyzes our deepest longing for love and meaning, stripping us of hope. It mocks our desirability: "No one wants you. No one enjoys you. You have no place with us. So just leave or bow down and serve us."

Contempt isolates its victims by branding them unworthy of love.

Who wants to be around a laughingstock? Mockery draws a line in the sand, separating its victim from the crowd. On the other side of the line is the in-group, laughing; near them is the silent crowd that will not risk stepping across the line to stand with the victim in his isolation.

After dividing and isolating, contempt withers hope by making its victim feel foolish, deadening desire.

A young woman attended a family gathering, dressed in a new outfit for the occasion. Her sister snapped: "Looks like you just walked out of one those ridiculously expensive catalogs." Instantly, she felt conspicuous and isolated—no one else had dressed the way she did. She began to doubt herself: "Maybe I spent too much on the outfit. Why can't I dress appropriately?" Her desire to be lovely, to be enjoyed for something as small as dressing attractively, seemed like a shrill inner voice joining in on her sister's taunt.

Part of the power of contempt is that it reverberates in the heart long after the words are spoken. Beyond the scornful words, the contemptuous question echoes, "Why can't I get the thoughts out of my mind?"

The event that provoked this young woman's self-doubt and loneliness was petty and small, but its relative insignificance made its power seem that much more worthy of contempt. She began to question, "What is wrong with me that an innocuous remark can spiral me into the throes of cracking like a broken pot?"

This is the unholy leverage of contempt: It renders desire foolish and painful, leaving the soul susceptible to the influence and control of others. Contempt then offers the option, "Join us or die. Be like us or face even greater mockery." The weakened, isolated, and exhausted heart is apt to give in to the force of contempt and join the ranks of the arrogant.

Contempt Shames and Destroys

I am a worm and not a man,
> scorned by everyone, despised by the people.

All who see me mock me;
    they hurl insults, shaking their heads.
"He trusts in the LORD," they say,
    "let the LORD rescue him.
Let him deliver him,
    since he delights in him."

Psalm 22:6-8

You have made us a reproach to our neighbors,
    the scorn and derision of those around us.
You have made us a byword among the nations;
    the peoples shake their heads at us.
I live in disgrace all day long,
    and my face is covered with shame
at the taunts of those who reproach and revile me,
    because of the enemy, who is bent on revenge.

Psalm 44:13-16

Under the exposure of scorn, the psalmist does not even feel human—he is a lowly worm. Others shake their heads in derision at his name; he is a bad joke. The psalmist covers his face in the horror of shame.

"Where is your God? Will *He* rescue you?" laughs contempt. *Am I a fool to trust God?* we wonder. It seems that not only has God allowed us to be reviled, but He may even be the one behind the assault. When we are exposed as trusting in a god that is unable or unwilling to save us, it gives rise to shame.

Contempt mocks the goodness of God. The haughty eyes of the arrogant seem to imply that God's eyes don't see; otherwise, why would He permit the mocker to scoff with impunity? What am I to hope in if God is unwilling to shut the mouth of the contemptuous? "How long will the enemy mock you, God? Will the foe revile your name forever?" (Psalm 74:10). What will life hold if the arrogant can mock God and apparently get away with it?

The arrogant usurp the throne of God and secure service with contempt. Power is only a small part of their desire, however. They enjoy the opportunity to see the weak crawl like a worm. One client commented, "I enjoy putting people down. I love to see a person speechless because they don't know what to say. I like to play with you until you know I am going to win; then I can walk away."

Even for those who are not so practiced at contempt, it is obvious that an air of indifference or nonchalance has the power to cut to the heart.

One woman said, "At times, I will do anything to get my husband in a fight, but when he responds with his nose in the air, indifferent to my attack, I go crazy." She was reflecting the cry, "Love me or hate me, but just don't contemptuously ignore me." To be ignored, treated with indifference, or haughtily patronized cuts to the quick and provokes strong fury. And in the protestation of fury, the contemptuous watch with wicked satisfaction as their victim grovels in rage and shame.

There is a malevolent joy in perpetrating harm that strengthens the illusion: "God does not see, therefore I am a god. And I can make others do more than serve me; I can make them pay for my pain." The contemptuous person will never be satisfied until he has humiliated his prey.

Why is the desire to destroy human dignity at the core of contempt?

Human dignity is a reflection of the glory of God, and it bears a beauty and an allure that supernaturally draws the heart to bow before God in worship and service. The evil one, and all who consciously or unwittingly serve him (at any one moment), hate glory: that bright, beautiful reflection of God's character. God's glory is unassailable; it cannot be tarnished or destroyed. But a derivative manifestation of His glory, human dignity, is free to be violated and ruined.

The power of contempt is that it assails beauty and tarnishes glory—claiming equal power to God without immediately facing God eye to eye.

At first blush, that assessment may seem too severe. When my wife asks if we can go for a walk and I snort, "Sure! And when am I supposed to get this project done?" am I really on the side of evil attempting to destroy glory? Or when my daughter asks if we can go out to eat and I retort, "You can't have everything you want, you know!" am I attempting to rob her of dignity? Of course I am—not as a final statement of my life desire, but in that particular moment I am siding with the evil one. His very name, "Satan," means the Accuser—the one who slanders with contempt.

Tragically, we use contempt daily without being aware of what we are doing. How does contempt spread its poison in our everyday encounters?

THE FACE OF CONTEMPT IN DAILY INTERACTIONS

Contempt shows its everyday face in all gossip, most boasting, and all blameshifting.

Contempt as Gossip

"Did you hear that Mr. Smith was caught in an affair?" We gasp in horror and relish more details. We love to know: to peek into the private moments, the heartache, the shame of others. Even more, we love to talk: to dissect with contemptuous precision the flaws and foibles of our prey caught in the web of our words. We feel smug satisfaction that we are not like them. In effect we have become their judge and jury, dishing out punishment with certainty and impunity. We are gods, conducting a parlor discussion on Mount Olympus.

Gossip is slander: accusing without recourse to defense, passing judgment without due process. It is soul murder. No wonder Paul places gossip in the list of the most heinous, God-hating sins perpetrated against people and God.[1]

Gossip occurs almost every time we speak negatively about another person. This is backbiting—we would never say in that person's presence what we speak in his or her absence. The ruling principle—"Have I said this to the person directly, and am I willing to say it again?"—helps distinguish legitimate conversation and prayer about others from defaming gossip.

Gossip also empowers through fostering perverse intimacy. This happens whenever we are "privileged" to be included in the inner sanctum of the gossiping storyteller. Gossips are gatekeepers of the community, who regulate reputations and can grant grace when we are ushered into their shadows. Their talk seems like delectable nourishment: "The words of a gossip are like choice morsels; they go down to the inmost parts" (Proverbs 18:8). Their power, however, lies in their ability to divide: "A perverse person stirs up conflict, and a gossip separates close friends" (Proverbs 16:28).

When we speak about others, do we hunger for their joy and sorrow for their struggle, or do we merely gain access to the storyteller as a result of listening and joining the conversation? This is another ruling principle for identifying gossip. If our conversation draws us to pray and engage in activity for their good, then our words are likely not the contemptuous slander of a gossip.

Contempt as Boasting

"My dad makes more money than your dad!"

"Oh yeah? Well, my dad can beat up your dad any day!"

The boast of young boys gives way in adult years to the quiet boasting of what kind of creature adorns the front of my shirt; what emblem is fastened to the front of my car; whom I had lunch with; how many responses I got on my most recent evangelism outing.

Status seeking, selfish ambition, and grandstanding are the contemptuous boasts of arrogance: "Look at me! Look at what I know, whom I know, what I can do, what others do for me!" Boasting may be insidiously subtle in adult years, but it is no less prevalent.

The Bible tells us that the arrogant—that is, all of us on occasion—boast about their power, their desires, their wealth, their cleverness, their future, and their abilities.[2] The core of their ungodly boast—"Glory in me"—is framed with contempt because they cannot bear for anyone else's glory to steal their limelight. All self-glory contains a contemptuous diminishment of others. Listen to most subtle boasts and you can hear the implied statement: "You are ignorant; you are not in the in-crowd; you are not as well-off."

Contempt is rooted in most of our conversations about others and about life. It is particularly present in all blameshifting.

Contempt as Blameshifting

"Why didn't you pick up the dry cleaning? You were right there!" Few criticisms are free of the smell of contempt. We often coat our expressions of pain, anger, and desire with contempt. If we don't, our words will open us to even greater vulnerability in the face of the offense we have already suffered.

If you hurt me, why would I want to open my heart to more pain after I express my first round of hurt? And so I address you with some hint of contempt in order to shield myself from greater pain.

If this is the case when we have been failed, it is even more the case when we are caught in failure. Our natural response when we are exposed as having failed is either to grovel in self-contempt or act out in other-centered contempt. Usually, the first response is called guilt and the second blameshifting. Both, however, are efforts to escape the raw sorrow of harm.

Self-contempt blames some flaw in the self rather than face the harm done to the other. Guilt is, in fact, a perversely self-centered effort to escape the wound and the potential for judgment. If I bruise myself sufficiently, then how dare you harm me or ask any more of me than the hatred I have already heaped on myself?

In other-centered contempt, the offender blames some flaw in the victim for the wound he has inflicted. The classic case is Adam's contemptuous assault of God. When exposed for violating God's command, he claimed, "The woman you put here with me—she gave me some fruit from the tree, and I ate it" (Genesis 3:12). Notice the order of the accusation: (1) God, You blew it. You created this woman—it's *Your* blunder. (2) She gave it to me; I didn't go after it. It's *her* fault. (3) (Finally, spoken more as an afterthought.) I *did* take a bite.

Contemptuous blameshifting violates God and others as we refuse to bear the weight of our offense with sorrow and strength. What does contempt gain for us in this situation? It blocks relational movement, deadening the desire of others to love us. When faced with contempt, most people flee or defend themselves with intensified anger. In either case, the one who uses contempt feels both safe from desire and free from the call to love and be loved. It is an apparently impenetrable shield that blocks any movement toward the heart.

What did contempt do for Adam? Momentarily, it allowed him to discount God's exposure of his sin and freed him from desiring a reality that would have been new to his experience—mercy.

MERCY AND CONTEMPT

Mercy is hard to endure. In fact, mercy is harder to receive than contempt. Both contempt and mercy strip away pretense and expose the heart, but mercy offers the exposed soul the opportunity to embrace desire and hope. For many, the prospect of hope is too great a desire to bear. It was for my (Dan's) friend Deb.

Deb is a victim of Satanic ritualistic abuse (SRA). For years, her life was adrift with secrets of such bitter horror that she refused to do anything but assault herself with alcohol, drugs, and food. She was hospitalized and treated with professional disdain and intolerance. In many ways, the hospital staff treated her with the same contempt and hatred she had felt in the cult.

After many tumultuous experiences, Deb encountered Christ and began to grow in grace and wisdom. Her history as well as her calling brought her the opportunities to interact with many other SRA victims in her church and to teach on the struggles of abuse. She became known as a powerful and articulate speaker on the issues ignored by professional helpers, who often overlook the data of ritualistic abuse.

One of Deb's speaking invitations came from a group of psychiatrists in the area where she had been hospitalized twenty years earlier. She accepted the invitation "to publicly shame the man whose in-patient facility did as much harm as the cult." She planned her revenge in detail.

Days before the opportunity came to seek blood, God convicted Deb of her sin in planning reprisal. However, although she was convicted, she was not broken: She decided not to expose the doctor but was unwilling to struggle with her hatred.

The opportunity to speak, which Deb had originally chosen as a forum for retaliation, turned out to be a great success. Many asked about her relationship with God. She spoke to eager and open psychiatrists who wanted to learn about Jesus. It was a miracle.

But she was further humbled. The man who had professionally treated her with treacherous contempt came to her and asked her forgiveness. He then shared with her the changes he saw in her life.

Deb was staggered by a flood of profound confusion and self-contempt. Why would God give her a powerful voice for good, when her heart was so drawn to wickedness? Why did God graciously gift her with her enemies' repentance after her heart had been so hard? After days of struggle, her heart lifted with the thought: "His mercy is greater than my contempt. He loves me, and He smiles with delight toward me."

God's kindness toward us is almost harder to bear than His apparent neglect or anger. His kindness requires us to let down our guard and receive—just when we are so sure that He will deposit a snake in our outstretched hand. No wonder Paul asks: "Do you show contempt for the riches of his kindness, forbearance and patience, not realizing that God's kindness is intended to lead you to repentance?" (Romans 2:4).

God in His holy strength is never thwarted by contempt—He mocks those who mock Him. In His odd mercy, however, He handles our contempt by cursing His own Son. Our contempt will never be shattered until we are unnerved by God's contempt toward the arrogant and we are drawn to the horror of the Father cursing the Son. Here we will see the divine about-face of contempt: from evil's mockery to the mockery of evil.

13

Holy Contempt:
The Mockery of Evil

The stand-up comedian rolled his eyes with disdain. He threw his head back with disgust as the words rolled out of his mouth, "Well, excuuuuse me!" We roared with delight.

Cool, hip contempt—mockery, cynicism, sarcasm—is the humor of our day. It draws us into laughter and flippant jousting with one another. Humor, spiced with a dash of contempt, can be enlivening.

Are we drawn to contempt and sarcasm because of the presence of sin in our hearts? Yes, but only in part. Contempt also arouses pleasure because it reflects something about the character of God that is often overlooked: God is a mocker.

God laughs with scorn at the obstinate folly of the arrogant. He ridicules with mockery and curses. Contemptuous mockery may be evil's weapon against the glory of God, but it is also His weapon of destruction, which will eventually crush all who oppose Him.

Our use of contempt against others and ourselves will be transformed to the degree that we are unnerved by God's mockery of arrogance and awed by the spectacle of the contempt He unleashes against His own Son.

GOD, THE MOCKER

Like anger, our contempt is not so much wrong as it is palsied and misdirected. We must learn to mock with God's perspective, boast in weakness, and taunt death and suffering with the confident laughter of trust. To do so, we must be unnerved by God's mockery of evil.

God Laughs

It is a frightening thought: God mocks. This is not our vision of God. We wish to see Him as gracious, kind, long-suffering, and occasionally—and only after lengthy provocation—angry.

We can barely imagine an angry God who disciplines us. But a contemptuous God, who is not just concerned about victory but who longs to shame His foe, is beyond our comprehension.

God does more than rage against arrogance; He plans on humiliating it. He laughs at evil:

> The One enthroned in heaven laughs;
>> the Lord scoffs at [those who rage against him].
> *Psalm 2:4*

> The wicked plot against the righteous
>> and gnash their teeth at them;
> but the Lord laughs at the wicked,
>> for he knows their day is coming.
> *Psalm 37:12-13*

God observes the deceit and rage of evil and laughs. But the laughter is not polite and pleasant. Does He laugh the way a parent might chuckle when he sees his child put on adult shoes and stagger around? No. God laughs with the kind of mockery that is staggering in its raw intensity.

God Ridicules

God's laughter is harsh. In one passage, He is depicted as making drunken Moab (a country near the Dead Sea in continual conflict with Israel) wallow in its vile debauchery:

"Moab's horn is cut off;
>   her arm is broken,"
>   declares the LORD.
"Make her drunk,
>   for she has defied the LORD.
Let Moab wallow in her vomit;
>   let her be an object of ridicule."
Jeremiah 48:25-26

Consider what God plans to do with Moab, a model of arrogant excess. He will let the vile by-product of sin (vomit) serve as the basis of the ridicule. Evil will get drunk to assert its arrogance, and then it will wallow in the rotten fruits of its foolishness. Once a proud nation, Moab will become an object of disgust and ridicule.

Paul drew forth this thought in poignant simplicity. "Do not be deceived: God cannot be mocked. A man reaps what he sows" (Galatians 6:7). God will not endure mockery. He told the people of God after their rebellion in the desert, "not one of them will ever see the land I promised on oath to their ancestors. No one who has treated me with contempt will ever see it" (Numbers 14:23).

God will not be mocked without consequences. Neither will He allow Himself to be mocked without turning the mocker into a laughing-stock. God does more than laugh and ridicule—He also humiliates.

God Humiliates

Laughter stings; ridicule pierces; but humiliation crushes pride. It's one thing to spill coffee on your clothing and realize that the people across from you are noticing and laughing. It would be further humiliating if they pointed at you and made derisive remarks. But it would be absolutely crushing if someone dumped the rest of the coffee in your lap and then threw you out of the restaurant.

In one of the most startling passages in the Bible, God sexually assaults whorish Nineveh and throws dung on her naked, exposed body, publicly humiliating her by exposing her idolatrous sin:

"I am against you," declares the LORD Almighty.
    "I will lift your skirts over your face.
I will show the nations your nakedness
    and the kingdoms your shame.
I will pelt you with filth,
    I will treat you with contempt
    and make you a spectacle.
All who see you will flee from you and say,
    'Nineveh is in ruins—who will mourn for her?'
    Where can I find anyone to comfort you?"
Nahum 3:5-7

God's assault makes us cringe. Does He not value fallen human dignity? Does He have no propriety? In a culture appropriately sensitized to the horrors of sexual abuse, this passage seems wanton and unconscionable.

Three considerations can help us understand the significance of this violent imagery.

First, *humiliation exposes the crime.* Nineveh's skirts are pulled over her head, exposing her nakedness. For years, Nineveh had been lifting her skirts to false gods and whoring on every hillside. Her nakedness was her pride; God was not the first to lift her skirts and expose her nakedness. But He is the first to expose the horror of her sin.

God shames the arrogant in those same places where they shamelessly flaunt their insolence. Pride comes before a fall: God's economy of contempt is to shame the very area that most adorns our sinful pride.

Second, *humiliation is poetic justice*. God pelts her with filth (the word is better translated "dung"). Nineveh is lovely—even as a pagan nation, she bears the image of the Creator and is pursued by God (see the book of Jonah). But she has used and pillaged God's beauty in herself and stolen the beauty of others. Because she despoils the glory of God, God covers the remnant of her beauty beneath dung. Since she is dirty, she will be covered in dirt. Poetic vengeance matches the meter of sin with the rhythm of shame.

Third, *humiliation provokes horror*. Humiliation is the final warning: Repent or be consumed by God's burning rage. It is also a warning to others: Flee or be humiliated. Those who pass by look at her naked, filth-covered body and recall her in her sensual, stunning prime. The gasp of horror is the same—"Who will comfort her?" Any attempt to comfort would only intensify the hemorrhaging shame. To be that exposed is to be beyond hope of consolation.

God will not be mocked. We are called to repent—or face His cruelest mockery. He will relentlessly expose our secret idolatries and our brazen arrogance. If our heart is willing to struggle to know Him, He will patiently reveal our need for Him. But if we turn our heart against Him and flaunt our sinful excess before heaven and earth, He will not hesitate to respond with severity.

We must shudder before His mockery. We must be horrified by our ongoing arrogance that shames our glory in self-contempt and violates glory in others with other-centered contempt—and, far more, we must shudder over our continuing defilement of God's glory.

To shudder is the prelude to grace. If we are horrified, then a crack inside of us opens to hear something even more inconceivable—

all the contempt that should be directed against our sin, God hurled at the glorious Son. Horror opens the door to wonder. And wonder is the invitation to worship.

GOD'S MOCKERY OF GOD

A pastor was sharing the gospel with a group of six hundred high school students. Normally an effective communicator, for some reason on this occasion he spoke poorly and failed to win his audience. The harder he worked, the more disjointed and ineffective he became. Perspiration ran down his face as he lost his place in his notes. Finally, his ordeal ended and he sat down.

The teacher who had invited him stood and publicly apologized for his confusing presentation. He wilted in a pool of shame.

Several weeks later, the pastor ran into a few of the students at a mall. One student called him over to a group of six long-haired, ear-ringed kids lounging around smoking cigarettes. He felt immediate shame, and the perspiration returned with the memory of his awful ordeal.

One kid spoke for the group: "Dude, you sucked smoke the other day." (Translation: *You were truly ineffective.*) "A lot of dudes dissed you, but you were righteous." (Translation: *A number of people found fault with you, but that did not keep you from being faithful to your calling.*) "We wanna hear how you do that church stuff, 'cuz we'd have punted if the sweat were hittin' the boards like it wuz for you." (Translation: *We want to know what you believe, because we are more controlled by shame than you seem to be.*)

His willingness to persevere in the face of mockery and shame enticed six kids to consider the gospel. It is the Lord's willingness to bear mockery and shame that moves us to the same wide-eyed wonder.

THE CREATION'S MOCKERY OF THE SON

All who see me mock me;
> they hurl insults, shaking their heads:
"He trusts in the LORD," they say,
> "let the LORD rescue him.
Let him deliver him,
> since he delights in him."

Psalm 22:7-8

Then the governor's soldiers took Jesus into the Praetorium
and gathered the whole company of soldiers around him.
They stripped him and put a scarlet robe on him, and then
twisted together a crown of thorns and set it on his head.
They put a staff in his right hand. Then they knelt in front
of him and mocked him. "Hail, king of the Jews!" they said.
They spit on him, and took the staff and struck him on the
head again and again. After they had mocked him, they took
off the robe and put his own clothes on him. Then they led
him away to crucify him. . . .

Those who passed by hurled insults at him, shaking their
heads and saying, "You who are going to destroy the temple
and build it in three days, save yourself! Come down from
the cross, if you are the Son of God!" In the same way the
chief priests, the teachers of the law and the elders mocked
him. "He saved others," they said, "but he can't save himself!
He's the king of Israel! Let him come down now from the
cross, and we will believe in him. He trusts in God. Let God
rescue him now if he wants him, for he said, 'I am the Son
of God.'" In the same way the rebels who were crucified
with him also heaped insults on him.

Matthew 27:27-31, 39-44

All of the people surrounding Jesus—Roman guards, common folks, religious leaders, thieves—mocked Him, and He neither turned His face away nor returned their attack (see 1 Peter 2:23). Instead, the steady, silent gaze of God only intensified the human fury to violate: "Why doesn't He speak? Why doesn't He come down from the cross? If He is who He says He is, then why doesn't He do something?"

Jesus quietly bore the contempt of His creation—He seemed to draw it forth by refusing to defend His person and prove His calling. He moves toward us with a gaze that unnerves our arrogance and unleashes our effort to silence His silent stare.

Contempt unleashed leads to feeling foolish. Consider the last time you lashed out in a contemptuous frenzy toward yourself or someone else. In the moment, it feels necessary and satisfying. But the by-product is futility, which arises when our burst of derision proves impotent to bolster our flagging self-esteem or relieve our shame. And so the shame intensifies.

The foolishness of contempt unleashed compels us to work harder to save face, which in turn spurs further contempt. But no matter how derisively we mock, we will never get what we need, what only humble repentance can gain: grace. Indulging in contempt will never assuage our hunger for forgiveness. Eventually, we will either give ourselves over to an inner hardness or grow exhausted with our own contempt.

The Son of God bears our contemptuous hatred in order to intensify our contempt and expose the petty, self-centered ugliness of our hearts. He bears the Father's contempt, on the other hand, in order to reveal the unimaginable goodness of the Father's heart.

THE FATHER'S MOCKERY OF THE SON

It is inconceivable that the clay pot should curse the Potter. Even more unthinkable is that God the Father cursed God the Son on the cross. Paul points to the scandalous deed: "Christ redeemed us from the curse of the law by becoming a curse for us, for it is written: 'Cursed is everyone who is hung on a pole'" (Galatians 3:13). Here Paul is quoting a passage from the Law: "Anyone who is hung on a pole is under God's curse" (Deuteronomy 21:23). God's curse is His voice of mockery—a shout of derision.

God chose to violate His Son in our place. The Son stared into the mocking eyes of God; He heard the laughter of the Father's derision and felt Him depart in disgust. In effect, the horror of judgment that God brought upon Nineveh, as prophesied in Nahum 3, was leveled against Jesus.

Something inside us shouts: "It cannot be. How could the Father curse His Son? How could the perfect, beautiful, pure Son be assaulted with the vile content of our souls? How could He take our place—how could He bear our sin?"

In a mysterious instant, the Father who loved the Son from all eternity turned from Him in hatred. The Son became odious to the Father. It is the most inconceivable moment in the history of time. Jesus submitted to it in order to redeem His people for His Father's glory: "'He himself bore our sins' in his body on the cross, so that we might die to sins and live for righteousness; 'by his wounds you have been healed'" (1 Peter 2:24).

The willingness of Jesus to bear the stripes of mockery opens our heart and draws us to see that God's contempt has been poured out on the perfect, unblemished Son of God. We will never look into God's eyes and see contempt or mockery. No matter how hard our heart becomes or how far we flee, the Father's response at our return is not cold, cruel, cutting eyes, but the open arms of One who knows joy, not contempt, toward us.

If our heart is (even a little) staggered by this good news, then how are we to live out our pardon from God's contempt?

The answer, in part, is to learn to mock evil. To mock like God, we must learn to violate evil by boasting in weakness and taunting death and suffering with the confident laughter of trust.

TAUNTING DEATH AND SUFFERING

"Blessed are those who mourn, for they will be comforted" (Matthew 5:4). "Where, O death, is your victory? Where, O death, is your sting?" (1 Corinthians 15:55).

Death is an impostor; hopeless sorrow, a deceiver. Both pretend to be more true than trust. The evil one uses death to force the question, "Can you trust a God who lets you and your loved ones suffer and die?" The evil one thrusts sorrow in our face and claims: "You are alone. No God exists—and if by chance He does, then He is impersonal and a brute. Trust only in what you can see. Give your life to what assuages pain and escapes death." There is a grain of truth in these accusations, for the data of life does not validate God's goodness unless we view it through the lens of the cross.

But the sorrow of disappointed desire need not lead us away from God in hopelessness. Instead, it can lead us toward God in an invitation to hope. Paul tells us in Romans 5 that we are to rejoice in suffering because it deepens character, character increases perseverance, and perseverance does not disappoint because those who run the race will see God's smile of love.

The laughter of trust mocks evil. And true laughter is a reflection of resurrected hope. We mock evil with expectant tears that do not deny the laughter of the cross.

While we were writing this book, we lost a good, good friend. He was mentor to both of us as well as colleague, confidant, and traveling partner to Tremper. His death deeply stung us. No man more richly encouraged or delighted in our success. His death was the loss of a father.

But our friend's death compels us to believe that One greater than

Dr. Raymond Dillard delights in us. Someone with an even deeper passion for our good, will commend us—some day. The loss still provokes tears, but each tear is a taunt, a confident boast—"Evil, you thought you won, you fool. You took a man of depth, wisdom, passion, and glory. But you have not taken away his life. He lived well—wonderfully well. His passion remains. His soul continues to draw us to our day."

To taunt death and sorrow is to let tears cut a path in the soul that deepens the flow of passion toward good. It is to weep deeply while simultaneously savoring the anticipation of the Day of Glory. It is to embrace trust over sight; passion over deadness. Those who weep will one day laugh, and the laughter of glory can be borrowed today to keep hope alive in the face of pain and death.

BOASTING IN WEAKNESS

But he said to me, "My grace is sufficient for you, for my power is made perfect in weakness." Therefore I will boast all the more gladly about my weaknesses, so that Christ's power may rest on me. That is why, for Christ's sake, I delight in weaknesses, in insults, in hardships, in persecutions, in difficulties. For when I am weak, then I am strong.

2 Corinthians 12:9-10

Paul's boast is in weakness, not in his education, gifts, calling, or success. Many of us have heard this lesson so often that we have been inoculated against its startling truth. To truly believe it—to actually live it—would radically alter the fabric of life.

What does it mean to boast in weakness? And how does boasting in weakness put us on the righteous side of God's mockery of evil?

Paul boasts in irony. Irony refers to the incongruity between what might be expected and what actually occurs. It is the literary style

167

of God. Evil offers strength, but it leads to death. God offers weakness, and it opens the door to life. God loves irony because He is the master of surprise.

The surprise of God is that His strength shows itself most profoundly not in our proficiency at making life work, but in our weakness. His glory is made known not through what appears glorious, but through the base, the lowly, the humble. Usually, the mystery of glory is revealed in those who seem least likely to bear the resplendence of humanity, let alone the grandeur of God.

God chose Paul—an arrogant, brilliant, obsessed, mean-spirited Jewish man—to take the gospel to the Gentiles. What a joke! Not only did He use the least likely, but then He implanted a thorn (no one has the slightest idea what it was) to humble him further. Paul became a fool—but fools are the ones God uses to shame the wise and the strong.

If God used predictable people and principles to change the heart, we would soon master the principle and reduplicate the people—and thus exclude Him from the process. He won't allow us to do this. Instead, He transforms us by the most surprising means and through the most unusual people. He does so as we boast in weakness, frailty, failure, and foolishness.

I (Dan) spoke recently with a single friend who had been stricken suddenly with multiple sclerosis. For weeks she was unable to walk, work, cook, bathe, or take care of the normal activities of life. Her church came to her assistance, particularly an older man who had recently been converted. For some reason, this grizzled ex-bouncer in his sixties who had been toughened by the meanness of life now became her ally. He fought for her. He brought others into her life to offer daily care and support. He offered a strong arm to lean on.

A year before the tragedy of her illness, I had told her I would pray that she would learn to glow in the enjoyment of her God-given femininity. She was a caring therapist and a good woman, but her heart was seared by years of self-contempt. She offered mercy, but it came from a desire to do good, not from the depths of knowing goodness. When her illness occurred, it obliterated the vestiges of her strength in herself. It made her ache with consuming desire.

The illness forced my friend to ask and receive care. Her grizzled friend was a lovely angel—the oddest sort, of course. His persistence humbled her. His strength softened her. His love exposed her self-contempt as a palsied means to avoid trust. When I saw her, she glowed. We wept and laughed. Weakness had won. Glory had been revealed in irony.

God uses tragedy—the unexpected reversal of hope and humility—to bring about repentant brokenness and redeemed hunger. In the boast of weakness, He reveals His character and His good plan for us.

God uses absurdity to mock our arrogant demand for control—He knows that trust reveals a glory wilder than anything we can conceive. God uses weakness and foolishness to shame the strong and the wise. He invites us to join His mockery of evil by learning to shame the arrogant through tears and laughter.

14

The Corrosive Power
of Human Shame

John trembled before his wife, Martha. He had just admitted to an affair with Martha's best friend. His head hung, and he refused to look into Martha's inconsolable eyes. Her fury was beginning to build to quench the tempest of shame. "Who else knows?" she hissed. The horror of exposure was even more consuming than the pain of betrayal.

Mark shook his head in disgust. It was his first date with the girl beside him, and they were waiting in line to buy movie tickets—a long line stretched far behind them. He had forgotten his wallet, and he had only three dollars in his pocket. His face reddened and his heart raced as he realized he was stuck—he couldn't bear asking his date to pay, and he didn't want to get out of line. He wished he could simply fly away from his predicament.

Janet smiled politely. She thanked her friend for pointing out the smudge of mascara that looked like a small bug in the corner of her eye. Her friend remarked, "When I'm rushed, I usually look like that too." Janet had had plenty of time that morning. She had even allowed herself the unusual pleasure of feeling pretty. *What a fool I am*, she thought.

A lingering threat in our everyday encounters and experiences, shame is an acid that strips us of our dignity and dissolves hope. No other emotion better portrays hell—the utter loss of intimacy, wonder, and joy. Its corrosive effect is so strong that it can mold our souls and shape the direction of our lives. Shame is so painful that we react against it perhaps more than any other difficult emotion—but we must face the dread of shame if we are to grow in hope and joy.

THE SIGNPOSTS OF SHAME

A Painful Absorption with Self

Shame creates an absorption with self that can make us feel as if we're drowning in quicksand. The self-awareness that comes with shame seems to shake brutally our very ground of being. Our core identity, the self, seems too ugly to face up to without dire consequences. Therefore, we contemptuously label the ugliness in terms of flawed dignity: I am stupid, fat, undisciplined, always late, never prepared.

A friend missed an appointment with me (Dan). When I saw him several days later he remonstrated, "I am so sorry. I am a jerk not only for forgetting, but I forgot to call after I remembered I missed our time. What an idiot!" Shame attacks the self in terms of its identity. "I am a . . ." is the syntax of shame.

In several places the Bible depicts the attack of shame on our core identity in terms of how it alters our countenance. Our face sets us apart from any other person. Shame is felt first in the face, which reddens and then loses radiance and vitality. Notice the imagery in this passage from Isaiah 29:22—"No longer will Jacob be ashamed; no longer will their faces grow pale."

The psalmists also portray the force of shame in its effect on our countenance:

> I live in disgrace all day long,
>   and my face is covered with shame.
> *Psalm 44:15*

> Cover their faces with shame, LORD,
>   so that they will seek your name.
> May they ever be ashamed and dismayed;
>   may they perish in disgrace.
> *Psalm 83:16-17*

To be covered with shame is to feel the self engulfed in something disgusting, even hideous. It may seem extreme, but the experience of shame feels like a prolonged, tortuous death.

Flight from Exposure

A second signpost of shame is hiding. Adam and Eve flew like hunted birds to the camouflage of the bushes. We fly to the sanctity of our inner world. We escape through the wish of invisibility, the fantasy of shrinking into the wall.

I (Dan) recently addressed a seminar audience with sloppy organization and rote conviction—it was awful. I labored, and the audience was bored. Exposed, I felt myself slipping into the quicksand of shame.

Thankfully, all bad talks end. A person approached me after the lecture and as we chatted, I slunk closer and closer to the edge of the platform, then off the platform, and then against the back wall.

Finally, the person asked: "Are you trying to leave?"

I gasped. Was it that obvious? I guess so. Externally, I was shrinking back from the audience and my poor performance. Internally, I was slipping into the cocoon of dissociation.

Shame prompts a flight to some self-created world of safe numbness. "Dissociation" is a fancy word that means, "I'm out of here. I'm going somewhere that offers an escape from my inner agony. I'll fly to the safety my own creation—a place without the pain or demands of God's world."

Like any other fear-based withdrawal, flight disproportionately perceives the enemy as far worse than it is: therefore, escape only intensifies the terror. And so flight from shame only increases shame, making the prospect of looking in the eyes of the other or at the ugliness of the self that much more incomprehensible. Consequently, all dissociation—that is, a flight to invisibility—will fail and require more aggressive methods to stem the hemorrhage.

Violence against Self and Others

A third signpost of shame is emotional or physical violence directed against the self or against the one who originally witnessed our fall. Violence is a blood offering to the dark demons of shame.

A man I (Dan) respect sadly told me about a painful discussion with his adolescent daughter. He was hurt by something she said, and he told her. Not only did she refuse to acknowledge her failure, but she chided her father for being too emotional and thin-skinned. He erupted in a shame-induced rage, screaming in wounded pride.

The encounter turned into a rapidly spiraling nightmare, ending in disaster. The daughter's original flippancy hardened into disgust, and the father turned her disgust against himself. He struck his chest so hard he bruised himself as he screamed: "What do I have to do to get you to see I am a human being? I hurt too!"

Shame lashes out to destroy the self and blind the observer. The assault can be under the breath with damaging words or out in the open with a handgun, directed against the self or the other. In either case, the desire is the same: kill the enemy.

And what is the enemy? What unleashes the profound fury of shame? The answer to this question depends on our view of the cause of shame. Does it arise from a sense of deficiency, inadequacy, or imperfection? Or is it rooted in a moral foundation—a failure of trust, a refusal to rely on something or someone outside of ourselves?

WHAT IS SHAME?

Shame is *the traumatic exposure of nakedness*—for example, when a person does something harmful (has an affair), commits a blunder (forgets a wallet), or is caught in some flaw of appearance (smudged mascara). This exposure occurs when we feel the lance of a gaze (either someone else's or our own) tearing open the various cultural, relational, or religious coverings we put on. What is revealed, we feel, is an inner ugliness.

And what lies below the "clothes" of conformity and acceptability that seems so ugly? It's more than simply the act itself (conducting an affair, forgetting a wallet, or smudging makeup); many people do these things without feeling shame. Shame is provoked by something deeper than just the exposed "ugliness."

A Sense of Deficiency or Foolishness

Our culture generally views shame as the by-product of poor self-esteem. It can be said with more sophistication—diffuse ego boundaries, narcissistic fracture, or inadequate sense of self—but it boils down to the fact that we feel bad about ourselves due to the failure of others to offer "good enough" care.

This view assumes that we are a composite picture of how others treat us. Since we live in a shame-based world, family, or marriage, therefore, we take on the "views" of others. Listen to what two lead-ing theorists consider the most important component in the forma-tion of shame:

> [A] shame-based system . . . give[s] the message that he is defective and inadequate as a human being; eventually, he becomes ingrained with a deep sense of "dysgrace."[1]

> To have shame as an identity is to believe that one's being is flawed, that one is defective as a human being.[2]

These views lead to the following perspective: "I am not bad; but, at times, I do bad things. If I can comprehend and accept the reality that I am good—I am essentially a lovable, lovely, pure being—then I can live in that confidence and be humbled (good shame) when I occasionally do things inconsistent with my true goodness."

Christians tend to add to this view, "I am a new creature. I am pure because I have been declared righteous and filled with the Spirit of God. Now I must live out my goodness, admitting the few flaws that creep into my flesh." Further, some people presume that if we embrace the totality of our goodness and avoid a "worm" theology full of shame-based negative thinking, sin will be a random, infre-quent experience.

Without question, we can affirm that a person who struggles with shame views the self as flawed and defective. It is equally irrefutable that we are affected by family or social systems that violate our dig-nity. But is this the core of shame? Is the issue this simple: We feel shame because our significant others shame us?

The Exposure of Foolish Trust
It is more biblically accurate to affirm that we feel shame when people treat us badly—or even when they treat us well—because *shame is*

rooted in our inherent preference to trust false gods rather than depend on God for each and every moment of our existence.

Consider a typical, relatively insignificant experience of shame. I (Dan) was caught up in conversation with a good friend. We were drinking coffee, and I was listening intently to him, enthralled by his story and his storytelling craft. Just as he reached a poignant moment, I put my coffee cup to my lips and missed. I had thought the cup was closer than it was, and my coffee spilled down the front of my shirt. My friend paused, startled, and I quickly pushed back my chair—in the process spilling his coffee on the table. I felt ashamed.

Why did I feel shame for this accident, instead of regret or sorrow for my clumsiness, the disruption of the story, and the inconvenience for us both? Is it possible that I was shamed rather than sorry because in the instant of "transgression" I sinned against my true god—looking good and not coming across like a fool? Clearly, my "transgression" was not a sin—but my shame was consistent with God's desire for that moment. In that instant, shame exposed what I trust in for "life."

Shame arises when we feel deficient, yes. But far more, we feel deficient and ugly when the god we (covertly and at times unconsciously) worship lets us down and reveals the foolishness of our idolatrous trust. Shame is not primarily an experience of feeling bad or deficient as it is the exposure of foolish trust in a god who is not God.

SHAME AND IDOLATRY

When I worship the idol of looking good, or being bright, or attaining power, I have put my hope in a god that has no power to rescue and redeem. That is not a problem until I need to be saved. Once I need help—after spilling coffee, or speaking poorly—the god I created sits silently. In its inactivity, it mocks my cry for help.

Shame exposes what we worship. Listen to these analyses of shame by a poet and a prophet:

> All who worship images are put to shame,
>   those who boast in idols—
>   worship him, all you gods!
> *Psalm 97:7*

> But those who trust in idols,
> who say to images, 'You are our gods,'
> will be turned back in utter shame.
> *Isaiah 42:17*

Is it possible that all our shame is due to idolatry? Let's consider the story of Sean, a man I (Dan) worked with who experienced profound shame every time he spoke or thought about the horror of past abuse.

Sean was sexually abused by his older brother. It might seem obvious that his shame is simply the tragic result of being degraded in an act that was not his choice or desire—the result of being made a victim. How is it possible that his shame is related to idolatry?

Again, the question must be asked: Why does Sean feel shame rather than sorrow for himself, and also for his brother?

Our work exposed Sean's hatred of weakness and desire. As a young boy, prior to the abuse, he had learned that life is cruel and disappointing. He toughened his heart and refused to want anything from anyone. The exception was his older brother. His older brother was athletic, handsome, and intelligent. Sean longed for his brother to notice his jump shot, his growing muscles, and his grades.

Occasionally, his brother gave him attention, and Sean's heart swelled with joy. One night, after spending hours together, his brother offered to teach him how to masturbate. During the instruction his brother told Sean to touch him, and Sean complied. He hated himself and his brother, but he felt desperate and compromised. He felt searing shame.

The origin of the shame that Sean felt was the exposure of the desperate trust he invested in his brother to provide what no person or thing can do—rescue and redeem. Rather than face the foolishness of trusting his brother as a god, Sean hated himself for his weakness and desire. He had exchanged his old idol—his brother—for a new and even more pernicious god: freedom from weakness and desire. Whenever he recalled the past abuse or experienced desire that seemed odd or excessive, he retreated into shame and then into vicious self-hatred.

Sean had worked for years with a therapist who had affirmed his right to desire and the validity of facing weakness and limitation. It had helped. He was less afraid of weakness and desire. Internally, however, Sean had become more self-sufficient and hard.

This hard-hearted response is a common by-product of viewing shame simply as a result of others' mistreatment of us—of their failures that heap shame on us. More often than not, this view leads to an essentially self-centered preoccupation with healing our wounds. Instead, if we understand shame as the exposure of foolish trust in gods who will inevitably fail us, we will be drawn toward a tender-hearted response that glories in the mystery of forgiveness.

This is no easy process, however. What keeps our hearts blind to the real cause of shame?

SHAME AND SELF-WORSHIP

Our culture declares, "Shame arises because I am a victim and I feel bad about myself." The Bible declares, "Shame arises because I am an idolater and I feel foolish when my idol topples."

Shame is the divestiture of self-glory. It is the loss of the god—the extension of the self—that holds our world together. Shame is an experience of being exposed as a fool.

Isaiah exposes the foolishness that underlies shame. The idolater fashions his own god out of the raw materials with which he provides for life's basic necessities:

> Half of the wood he burns in the fire;
>> over it he prepares his meal,
>> he roasts his meat and eats his fill.
> He also warms himself and says,
>> "Ah! I am warm; I see the fire."
> From the rest he makes a god, his idol;
>> he bows down to it and worships.
> He prays to it and says,
>> "Save me! You are my god!"
>
> *Isaiah 44:16-17*

Isaiah's mockery is brutal. He portrays the idolater as a fool. We can almost hear the fool exulting, "Oh, man, am I cold—good thing I have the power to create warmth! And I need food—but I've got the power to satisfy my hunger. Let's see, what else? Oh, yeah—I also need a god who will comfort, protect, and save me. Hey—since I have the power to create fire and food, why don't I just make a god who will nourish my soul?"

It seems incomprehensible. How could anyone bow down and serve a god made out of his own labor, an extension of himself? Yet many of us prize our own creations—whether they're objects fashioned from wood or words—not as tools in service to a larger good, but as mere extensions of ourselves. Nothing is wrong with creative labor, but whenever an object of creation is prized as a delight that glorifies the creature-creator rather than the Creator, idolatry is at work.

In idolatrous worship, we are exalting self-sufficiency and self-determining power. An idol is really nothing more than an object or idea or desire that allows the creator to worship himself. Shame arises when worship—the ascribing of glory and honor—is invested in the self rather than in God.

"How long will you people turn my glory into shame?" God entreats. "How long will you love delusions and seek false gods?" (Psalm 4:2). Where do we look for glory? The great delusion of idolatry is that we can find rapture in ourselves—and therefore gain both exhilaration in and control over our god. Since the creation reflects God's glory, worshiping the creature allows us to counterfeit true worship without bowing before the glory of God.

The idolater knows he is not worshiping God. In fact, at some core level, the idolater recognizes that in worshiping his car, bank account, art work, freedom, reputation, service, he is worshiping himself. The object of his desire is little more than a symbol of his own grandiose self. But he hides his self-worship in the sweat and busyness of commerce and creativity. His idol-making is a thinly veiled glorification of his desire, but he refuses to face the shameful idiocy of his labor.

Does this sound extreme? If so, stop and consider how easily we slip into idolatry.

A godly man admitted to worshiping the god of debt reduction. After laboring for twenty years to pay off his mortgage, he succeeded. In tears he confessed, "I have never felt so empty. I thought I would be on top of the world, but I realize the dream of paying off my mortgage was a passion more important to me than pursuing righteousness."

How often do we trust our finances, health, reputation, children, and physical appearance to satisfy our souls more than God? That's how often we engage in idol-making.

SHAME AND IGNORANCE

Shame is an internal wake-up call—we are worshiping a god who is not God. But most idolaters are oblivious to their idolatry, and therefore they are hardened to feeling shame. Isaiah indicates that those who pursue idols escape the torment of shame by opting for blindness, ignorance, and delusion:

> All who make idols are nothing,
>   and the things they treasure are worthless.
> Those who would speak up for them are blind;
>   they are ignorant, to their own shame. . . .
> No one stops to think,
>   no one has the knowledge or understanding to say,
> "Half of it I used for fuel;
>   I even baked bread over its coals,
>   I roasted meat and I ate.
> Shall I make a detestable thing from what is left?
>   Shall I bow down to a block of wood?"
> Such a person feeds on ashes; a deluded heart misleads him;
>   he cannot save himself, or say,
>   "Is not this thing in my right hand a lie?"
> *Isaiah 44:9, 19-20*

Idolatry is sneaky worship. It is worship of the self, but it doesn't look that way at first. It appears more like a poor self-image. Or it looks like an insecurity that necessitates always looking good, or never making mistakes, or determination to be successful. Indeed, the object of idolatrous service is often something good. There is nothing wrong with carving a beautiful statue or polishing a cherished car. The danger is in the delusion, the blindness, and the ignorance in the belief that the object has the power to give life.

Blindness preserves the fiendish passion to retain power and glory. It offers the simple solution, "what I don't see, I don't have to deal with." As long as we ignore shame or consign it to a mere by-product of feeling bad about ourselves, our ignorance of idol-making will lead us to resolve shame by returning to the very thing that caused our shame in the first place—pursuit of our own glory.

Eventually, God in His kindness pierces the delusion. Shame has the power to shatter the glory of the voiceless, sightless god. When shame penetrates, it leads either to repentance or to annihilation.

SHAME AND CHANGE

Shame not only exposes idolatry, it also intensifies the cry of the soul. Shame pushes the heart to the extremity of life and death; tragically, shame usually edges the heart toward death.

Shame has the potential to arrest passion, close down desire, and turn the heart away from sorrow. Once passion, desire, and sorrow are dormant, the heart freely returns to idolatry without thought or feeling.

It is safer to feel shame (no matter how painful or destructive) than to feel sorrow. This is because shame closes down the heart and refuses to groan; sorrow increases momentum to seek, knock, and ask.

When I spilled the coffee on my shirt, I felt shame and allowed it to rob me of sorrow on two levels: (1) sorrow over loss, and (2) sorrow over sin.

Because of my clumsiness, I lost the pleasure of hearing a master storyteller weave his craft—we were so near the consummation of the story. The interruption felt like an unwanted phone call at an inopportune moment, breaking a spell that could not be conjured back at will. Although the disruption of the story was not the end of the world, it was nevertheless sad—even a small rip exposes the deeper fissures in existence. Shame masked my sadness over the loss. Rather than admit the loss, it was easier to wallow in shame and punishing contempt.

A second level of sorrow numbed by my shame involved the conviction of sin. The sin was not in the spill. It was not in the initial embarrassment, nor even in the growing shame. Rather, it was in my demand to be competent, adroit, and attractive. I deepened my sin as I opted for the numbing withdrawal of shame rather than facing my sorrow over my own idolatry revealed.

Shame need not lead us to withdrawal, however. It can incite confusion and passion. It can move us to ask and seek and knock on the door of God's mysterious heart. It can compel us to stand naked and cry out for wisdom. The psalmist portrays what is possible when instead of being numbed by shame, we allow it to open us to the deepest questions of our hearts:

> You have made us a reproach to our neighbors,
>> the scorn and derision of those around us.
> You have made us a byword among the nations;
>> the peoples shake their heads at us.
> I live in disgrace all day long,
>> and my face is covered with shame
> at the taunts of those who reproach and revile me,
>> because of the enemy, who is bent on revenge.
> All this came upon us,
>> though we had not forgotten you;
>> we had not been false to your covenant. . . .
> Awake, Lord! Why do you sleep?
>> Rouse yourself! Do not reject us forever.
> Why do you hide your face
>> and forget our misery and oppression?
> We are brought down to the dust;
>> our bodies cling to the ground.

Rise up and help us;
    rescue us because of your unfailing love.
Psalm 44:13-17, 23-26

An experience of shame will change our hearts. Either it will compel us to shut down, or it will draw us to cry out to God in shock, confusion, and desire. When we do battle with Him, He reveals His scandalous willingness to be shamed on our behalf. In rage we accuse Him; He turns to show us the disgraceful wounds of His own suffering. Shame, more than any other emotion, opens to us the strange heart of God.

15

The Redemptive Power of Divine Shame

Sacrificial love is unnerving. To be loved at great cost may provoke gratitude, awe, and a desire to honor, but it can also draw forth confusion or shame.

Some time ago I (Dan) was skiing with my middle child, Amanda. It was the end of the day and we were on an icy run. She was ahead of me by about twenty-five yards, and I was hanging back to make sure other skiers did not power by me and inadvertently run into her. I was watching closely as we came to a steep section and, as I feared, she hit a patch of ice and took a hard fall.

I raced to her to see if she was hurt and, without thinking, I hit the same patch of ice. My skis lifted off the ground and I collided with her small body. I hit her so hard I knocked the air out of her. As she gasped in pain and confusion, I picked her up and held her in my arms, saying over and over again, "Amanda, I am so sorry." I felt terrible shame.

She looked into my eyes and said through her sobs, "Daddy, I forgive you. I know you would never mean to hurt me." I felt helpless. I would never intentionally hurt her, true, but there was nothing I could do to take away her pain.

The shame of losing control and then harming someone I love tortured me, but her grace intensified my shame even more. Why?

Grace requires us to let go of our god of self-sufficiency. Our pride compels us to rectify a wrong, but grace exposes our inability to make it better. We are the helpless recipients of kindness.

When we are humbled in the presence of kindness, the experience of helplessness usually provokes a battle to regain control. I wanted to flee in shame, but Amanda's kindness did not allow me to escape. Shame leads to self-absorption, hiding, and hateful contempt. My daughter wanted me to join her in heart and soul, not to withhold myself. Her eyes invited broken sorrow, trust, and gratitude. What she wanted is similar to what the Lord desires.

SHAME AS AN INVITATION TO GRACE

Shame is an exposure of our idolatry. We are exposed in our foolish trust in ourselves when we are shamed because we spilled a drink on our lap, because a child makes poor grades, because our business flounders in mediocrity, because our spouse leaves us for a younger and more attractive person.

But shame is also a great gift. It can reveal sin and draw forth desire. If we honor shame as a severe mercy that can lead us to the wonder and wholeness of worship, then we need not fear (unto death) what will be drawn forth in the staggering moment of exposure. We can face shame as an invitation to look into the eyes of the One who does not condemn—but instead, He offers grace, forgiveness, and freedom.

Our ability to accept shame as a gift will grow to the degree that we are dumbfounded by a God who emptied Himself and bore disgrace for the sake of freeing us from idolatry. We encounter God's humiliation in His Son's incarnation, earthly suffering, and crucifixion. What are we to learn from His willingness to be humbled by shame?

THE HUMILIATION OF GOD

In the Incarnation

Immanuel, God with us—in human flesh. It is inconceivable. The foolishness of God becoming a man pervades even the environment of His birth: in poverty, in a lowly place, unattended except by beasts and shepherds, pursued by an evil king. Not exactly a royal entrance. The enfleshing of God is an offense to the Jews and a stumbling block to the Gentiles.

To our fallen minds, the idea of the Incarnation is more absurd than the idea of worshiping an idol of our own creation. It's far easier to believe that something seen can become unseen, than to believe that something unseen can become flesh. We can more easily believe that a creature can become a god, than to believe that God became a creature.

How can the eternal being become finite, frail flesh? The infinite Word, the second member of the Trinity, freely emptied Himself of glory and took upon Himself the limitations of humanity—but without sin. He did not cease to be God, but He humbled Himself in becoming like us and bearing physical hunger, exhaustion, and temptation.

Jesus submitted to the effects of being a creature—needing to gain nourishment for His body through food and for His soul through faith. He was not absorbed with His rightful prerogative to remain in glory, but He chose to enter the sorrow of a sinful world and become human. He submitted to the shame of humility and lowliness. We are invited to enter into His humility by allowing our hearts to be grieved and broken through the exposure of sin.

In Suffering

Although Jesus suffered throughout His earthly life, He did not turn from His Father. The path of obedience was the way of passion and suffering. He was assaulted by the evil one, ignored and mocked by His creation, and misunderstood by His own disciples. Berkhof points out the unique nature of Jesus' suffering:

> His capacity for suffering was commensurate with the ideal character of his humanity, with His ethical perfection, and with His sense of righteousness and holiness and veracity. No one could feel the poignancy of pain and grief and moral evil as Jesus could.[1]

It is no small matter that Jesus began His earthly ministry with the temptation to fill His empty stomach (pain), regain the kingdoms of His creation (glory), and experience the tangible hand of God protecting Him (sight versus trust). At the end of His ministry, He was tempted again to avoid the agony of the cross (pain), demonstrate His power (glory), and be rescued by a legion of angels (sight versus trust).

Jesus submitted to the shame of temptation and suffering without threatening or reviling those who harmed Him, entrusting Himself to the One who judges rightly. We are invited to face shame by entrusting our souls to God, our Advocate.

In Death and Crucifixion

Jesus physically succumbed to the great enemy: death. He was vanquished by the evil one, and for a moment drank the Father's wrath when the Father turned from the Son in sorrow and anger.

The picture of Jesus' death offered by C. S. Lewis in the Chronicles of Narnia series is chilling. Aslan, the lion, has been tied to the table. His mane is shorn. The banshees of hell shrill in mockery and joy:

the king has been vanquished. The knife is drawn, and the blood is spilt. The lion submits. He dies. The kingdom belongs to the rabble, and they celebrate by singing and dancing in drunken revelry.

It is nearly impossible to visualize the account without feeling the horror of vanquished shame. Our trust is betrayed, our hope shattered—our God has been defeated. We can hear the rounds of laughter—"Where is your God? If He is God, then let Him save Himself!"

Satan's laughter is an awful assault. It is nothing, however, compared to the estrangement of the Father and the Son. The deepest shame of the cross is the breaking of divine fellowship due to the ugliness of sin. The Son became sin; the Father cannot look on sin without hatred. The Son willingly took our place of condemnation—and for an instant, He bore the fury of God.

Why would anyone willingly choose to bear such a penalty for another's sin? The writer of Hebrews tells us:

Let us run with perseverance the race marked out for us,
fixing our eyes on Jesus, the pioneer and perfecter of faith.
For the joy set before him he endured the cross, scorning its
shame, and sat down at the right hand of the throne of God.
Hebrews 12:1-2

Jesus endured the shame of the cross because of joy—joy in glorifying His Father, and joy in redeeming His brothers and sisters (see Hebrews 2:11-12). We are invited to bear His disgrace and offer ourselves as a sacrifice of praise to God's glory and goodness.

THE PARADOX OF SHAME

When you were dead in your sins and in the uncircumcision
of your flesh, God made you alive with Christ. He forgave

us all our sins, having canceled the charge of our legal
indebtedness, which stood against us and condemned us;
he has taken it away, nailing it to the cross. And having
disarmed the powers and authorities, he made a public
spectacle of them, triumphing over them by the cross.
Colossians 2:13-15

Paul implies that there is a twist in the story of God's death.
The hero appears vanquished; it seems impossible for Him to save
Himself, let alone rescue us. The evil one's victory appears seamless.
The victory of evil is short-lived, however, for resurrection interrupts
the celebration of evil and triumphs over shame by introducing hope
into the universe.

Paul is singing a victory song. Evil has been made a shameful
spectacle, triumphed over by the redemption of God's humiliation.
Jesus willingly endured the shame of the cross, but He scorned it—
or, in other words, He shamed shame, because He refused to mistrust
His Father. His obedience to the Father shattered the power of the
evil one's kingdom. Under the onslaught of the greatest accusatory
contempt the evil one could muster, Jesus did not fail to trust His
Father. He actually seemed to look forward to evil's effort to shame
Him. Listen to the Suffering Servant:

I offered my back to those who beat me,
   my cheeks to those who pulled out my beard;
I did not hide my face
   from mocking and spitting.
Because the Sovereign LORD helps me,
   I will not be disgraced.
Therefore have I set my face like flint,
   and I know I will not be put to shame.

He who vindicates me is near.

    Who then will bring charges against me?

    Let us face each other!

Who is my accuser?

    Let him confront me!

Isaiah 50:6-8

The Suffering Servant did not hide; neither did He attack those who violated Him. He entrusted Himself to the One who would help Him and deepened His resolve to accomplish the purpose set before Him. Therefore, He was able to taunt the threat of shame: "Come attack Me, accuser! Face Me, eye to eye, and hit Me with your best shot. But your blows are impotent because I have an Advocate who will vindicate Me of every charge you level against Me."

Jesus did not turn to another god to find relief or strength; therefore, He did not fear shame.

If shame is the exposure of idolatry, then it is possible to trust in the true God and experience profound attack, assault, failure, and humiliation without succumbing to the inner hopelessness of shame.

What is the path that will enable us to break the power of shame? How can we taunt evil and death with the freedom of one who is not bound to shame?

FREEDOM IN SHAME

This side of glory, we will never be free of shame. In fact, Scripture indicates that those who are free from shame are the most arrogant and God-hating.[2] As with other difficult emotions, we can't simply resolve shame and heal it. But we can hear it.

As long as we are tempted to engage in idol-making, shame will linger—and we can profit from our experience of it. Each time we are caught in the throes of worshiping a god that is not God, we are invited to a process that leads to increased wonder and worship. This process occurs as we counter the self-absorption of shame with redemptive sorrow. As my heart grieves over the damage wrought by my endless pursuit of idols, I will grow free of the stinging self-consciousness of shame.

Shame exposes our ugliness and leaves us open to the attack and derision of the evil one. Sorrow opens the heart to the desire for redemption. And redemption always comes from outside of the self; therefore, the effect of redemptive sorrow is to increase hope. When shame exposes us, we can counter our penchant to hide in self-protection by hoping in an Advocate who will protect us and come to our defense.

Confident hope increases gratitude. The light of gratitude melts shame in all its violent, furious self-hatred. As sorrow and hope open the door to the wonder of worship, worship draws forth our expressions of gratitude for God's goodness.

The path that enables us to break the power of shame leads us through humility (sorrow), hope (confidence), and gratitude (worship).

Freedom in Humility: The Desire for Redemption

"In you, LORD my God, I put my trust" (Psalm 25:1). Humility consists in the simple acknowledgment that all my idols are vain and useless. They are ridiculous scams that mean nothing. Shame holds little power in the heart of a broken person whose false gods are (even temporarily) shattered. Listen to a man who was not controlled by shame:

The tax collector stood at a distance. He would not even look up to heaven, but beat his breast and said, "God, have mercy on me, a sinner."

I tell you that this man, rather than the other [the shame-
less Pharisee], went home justified before God. For all
those who exalt themselves will be humbled, and those who
humble themselves will be exalted.

Luke 18:13-14

The tax collector was not consumed with himself. He was
not worried about how he looked or whether he was an object of
derision—deeper matters of the soul were more important.

A humble heart cries out to God, aware that it is undeserving,
hungry, and full of sorrow. There can be no true biblical humility
without sorrow. Sorrow is a wail of desire that cuts through the din of
self-absorption. It intensifies our hunger for what we most desire, and
what no idol can provide: forgiveness, redemption, and reconciliation.

I (Dan) spoke to a man who lived his life with the pompous
illusion of power. He was wealthy, attractive, and esteemed in his
circle of society. But high society is no buffer against severe family
problems, and this man's life was shattered when his favored daughter
took her life. He could not escape the horror of his loss. Further, his
pain opened his heart to see the vain, utterly useless squandering of
his life in society intrigue and power-brokering. His sorrow cut a
channel in his heart that allowed the water of God to overwhelm him
with conviction and then nourish him with the relief of forgiveness.

Sorrow exposes where we turn to find life. To whom or what do
we lift our souls? Many believe in Christ for forgiveness of sin and the
promise of heaven, but they live their lives in the illusory refuge of their
own power. The fruit of redemption, however, is displayed in a broken
heart. Our hearts are broken as we acknowledge our sin, admitting our
helplessness to battle our enemies or stand righteously before God.

Brokenness is the antidote to shame. The power of shame is never
crushed by affirming our goodness or dignity; instead, it is melted in
sorrow when we are overwhelmed by what it exposes in our hearts.

Repentant sorrow comes as we pursue shame beyond its horizontal cause (skiing into my daughter) and taste the tragic consequences of its idolatrous foundation (foolish trust in my strength to stay in control and keep from harming others).

Sorrow, in turn, lifts our heart before the One we have offended, in hunger for what seems inconceivable, given our condition: restored relationship. Any approach to shame that does not deepen our need for repentant sorrow will lead to a self-absorbed focus on ourselves rather than a greater confidence in grace.

Freedom in Hope: Confidence in an Advocate

> In you, LORD my God,
>> I put my trust.
> I trust in you;
>> do not let me be put to shame,
>> nor let my enemies triumph over me.
> No one who hopes in you
>> will ever be put to shame,
> but shame will come on those
>> who are treacherous without cause.

Psalm 25:1-3

Sorrow opens the heart to recognize the depth of desire that no god can satisfy. However, it does not resolve the emptiness of an exposed, naked heart. To keep the heart from fleeing in abject fear, it must be able to trust in an Advocate.

A child gets pushed around by older boys. His face is shoved in the dirt; he is taunted and shamed. The boys depart with arrogance. When they are a half-block away, the shamed boy regains a shred of dignity as he shouts: "You just wait! You wait until my big brother finds out what you did to me. We'll see if you're laughing then." He turns to an advocate in his effort to protect his fragmented heart.

Trust in an Advocate shatters shame because it draws us to look beyond the hopelessness of the moment and gaze on the One whose strength and love is capable of pulling us out of the mire.

Hope is a loan from the past and the future, enabling us to deal with the debt of the present. Our faith is centered in the past—the death and resurrection of Jesus. Our hope is centered in the future—the glorious return of Jesus, the death of death, the shattering of all shame, and the redemption of His people. When we are assaulted by contempt, it is our trust in redemption that allows us to confront, mock, and shame shame.

The shame of exposed foolishness is the door through which the evil one scurries to malign and torment our hearts. The contempt of shame reflects the whispers of evil that seduce us to believe we are alone and too stained for grace.

A man I (Dan) respect struggles with occasional homosexual fantasies. He is a faithful husband, committed father, and gifted pastor. No one in his congregation has the slightest idea of his battle. If he shared his burden, he would likely be fired. For decades he hid in silence, cloaking his struggles from everyone.

Over many years, he faced the hold that a spectrum of idols had over his soul. With wisdom and circumspection, he allowed his heart to be known by a few friends, including his wife. His shameful silence was broken by sorrow, and his empty heart was filled with a new sense of advocacy by the Spirit of God.

He told me that many times before he preaches, he can sense the accusations of evil: "You are disgusting. You have no right to open up the Word of God. Quit, you faggot." But he has chosen to remain faithful to his calling because of the advocacy of the Spirit and the presence of a few close friends who grieve over his battle but believe in his calling. He is not alone. Shame does not rule over him in silence.

The Bible assures us, "There is now no condemnation for those who are in Christ Jesus" (Romans 8:1). In hope we hear the whisper of God's delight: "You are loved. You are called to live out truth. Persevere; you are mine."

My friend still struggles with occasional bouts of fantasy, but he has found that the hope of heaven is searing the bonds of shame. He is stained, but hope draws him to glimpse a vision of what he will one day become. His anticipation of glory—a day of full, rich, pure pleasure—has weakened the power of the idolatrous lust and enabled him to look the accusations in the eye and say: "He who vindicates me is near. Who then will bring charges against me? Let us face each other! Who is my accuser? Let him confront me!" (Isaiah 50:8). In hope, he has shamed shame. It has opened his heart to moments of grateful, awe-inspired worship.

Freedom in Gratitude: The Wonder of Worship

Remember, LORD, your great mercy and love,
    for they are from of old.
Do not remember the sins of my youth
    and my rebellious ways;
according to your love remember me,
    for you, LORD, are good.

Psalm 25:6-7

As sorrow opens our hearts to redemptive desire, it halts our long fall into destructive self-absorption. Hope in our Advocate opens hearts to confidence, and confidence stops the fearful flight of shame. Gratitude softens the self-hatred of shame.

The violence of shame prefers to annihilate the self rather than allow it to live in hellish loneliness. It is a soul suicide that defends the last thread of dignity behind a roar of rage.

Hatred is like a huge, muscle-bound bully that refuses to allow anyone to get near the stricken, bloodied soul. The bully is cruel, offensive, and antagonistic. He compels others to flee or fight. Either response works to justify more hatred. It is a vicious defense that refuses to cry out for an advocate who will redeem.

The only path through this ferocious defense is a goodness that neither attacks the bully nor fears him. Instead, it offers the bully what he really desires: forgiveness and reconciliation. This is how gratitude softens the self-hatred of shame.

Nearly three decades ago, Tremper offered a bully a taste of redemption. Tremper and I first met in a music class in eighth grade. I was a bully. A number of years of sexual abuse at the hands of a Scout master and by camp counselors at a boys' camp had strengthened a deep vein of rage and hatred in me.

During the music class, Tremper tapped me on the shoulder to ask if he could borrow a comb. I was a mean kid. I grabbed him by the shirt and hauled him out of his desk.

Tremper's response was to laugh. Never in my young life had I experienced something so disconcerting. I was a large, aggressive football player with a bad reputation who used intimidation to hide a deep hatred for myself and an utter terror about relating to others. But Tremper laughed—a guileless, kind, contempt-free laugh. It melted me instantaneously. As far as I was concerned, from that point on we were best friends. Our friendship became the means by which God cornered me long enough for me to hear and respond to the gospel.

Gratitude arises in a heart that is stunned by the lover's pursuit in spite of countless reasons to attack or withdraw in disgust. As Paul said, it is the kindness of God that leads to repentance (Romans 2:4). Gratitude arises the instant that grace is received; it is a praise of thanksgiving that is full of wonder and irony. How could someone choose me when my heart is so ugly and hard? It makes no sense. It violates my expectations, yet it arouses the deepest chords of desire.

Shame has no power in a heart that is full of thanksgiving. Hatred stands no chance in a heart that sings with innocent desire, humble sorrow, solid hope, and grateful praise to God's goodness.

David, the writer of so many psalms, gives us a wild picture of worship that is free from shame. As David returned the Ark of the Covenant—a symbol of the presence of God—to its proper place among the people of God, he danced, praised, and worshiped God with a heart that was flooded with joy in being chosen to be in the presence of God:

> Wearing a linen ephod, David was dancing before the LORD with all his might, while he and all Israel were bringing up the ark of the LORD with shouts and the sound of trumpets.
>
> As the ark of the LORD was entering the City of David, Michal daughter of Saul watched from a window. And when she saw King David leaping and dancing before the LORD, she despised him in her heart. . . .
>
> When David returned home to bless his household, Michal daughter of Saul came out to meet him and said, "How the king of Israel has distinguished himself today, going around half-naked in full view of the slave girls of his servants as any vulgar fellow would!"
>
> David said to Michal, "It was before the LORD, who chose me rather than your father or anyone from his house when he appointed me ruler over the LORD's people Israel— I will celebrate before the LORD. I will become even more undignified than this, and I will be humiliated in my own eyes. But by these slave girls you spoke of, I will be held in honor."
>
> *2 Samuel 6:14-16, 20-22*

Michal tried to shame David by pointing out that even the poorest and least of all the people—slave girls—saw his nakedness and passionate worship. He responded by recalling the honor of being chosen by God to rule, to celebrate. He faced the likelihood of even bearing greater shame, but the specter of shame was not a terror in a heart that rejoiced in worship.

Grateful worship begins with our acknowledgment of God's untold goodness in pouring out His mercy and remembering us in His kindness, not in our sin. A grateful heart has no need to engage in self-destruction through violent self-hatred. Self-hatred tries to annihilate what it assumes is the cause of shame—the self. Worship acknowledges that the cause of shame—idolatry—has been forgiven. Why would we turn on ourselves (or others) in vicious hatred when God's goodness reigns over us like a glorious rainbow?

As worship confirms for us that we are forgiven, we are freed from the fear of exposure. Worship, therefore, leads to freedom. It also leads to service, as we become free to join God in putting evil to shame.

FREEDOM TO SERVE

God is a God of irony. He delights in disrupting the sinful confidence of man. He chose for His Son to be born in shame, live His life in shame, and then die in the most shameful manner. Shame is evil's greatest weapon against God. But God takes the weapon of evil and uses it to mock and then destroy evil.

It is no less ironic that He intends for us to do the same thing. We are to join God in the paradox of using the weapons of evil to destroy evil: "God chose the foolish things of the world to shame the wise; God chose the weak things of the world to shame the strong" (1 Corinthians 1:27).

We are to shame the world by reveling in the beauty of weakness. Here is the paradoxical ground where God's strength is revealed: we are to rejoice in foolishness, because through it God's wisdom shames the wise.

For most people, shame is an enemy. For God's people, it becomes a friend that exposes our idolatry, draws us to the wonder of the Cross, and serves as a weapon to mock evil. A friendship with shame enables us to surprise the world with love. It also frees us to love one another with the love of God.

Once shame has lost its sting, we are freer to forsake the safety of our walled cities and venture into the hope of another city—the City of God. Bearing disgrace and rejecting safety for the hope of what will one day be ours energizes praise, promotes good, and pleases God:

> Let us, then, go to him outside the camp, bearing the disgrace he bore. For here we do not have an enduring city, but we are looking for the city that is to come.
>
> Through Jesus, therefore, let us continually offer to God a sacrifice of praise—the fruit of lips that openly profess his name. And do not forget to do good and to share with others, for with such sacrifices God is pleased.
> *Hebrews 13:13-16*

God loves paradox. He bears shame to make a spectacle of evil on the Cross. He invites us to bear disgrace in order to befuddle a world terrified of shame.

In understanding our deepest emotions, we enter into a fuller understanding of the God we worship. What kind of God do we worship? What kind of Being takes every dark emotion and turns it against Himself for our sake? As we glimpse Him through our struggles with anger, fear, jealousy, despair, contempt, and shame, we are pointed to the great mystery of who God is and how He works in our lives.

16

The Mystery of God

How astonishing that God chooses to give us a glimpse of Himself—however tarnished or imperfect the picture is to us—through allowing us to grapple with difficult emotions. As we seek a deeper grasp of our own emotions—anger-fear, jealousy-despair, and contempt-shame—the struggle opens our vision to see in fresh ways the heart of God.

The Scriptures, particularly the Psalms, reveal with startling clarity that our emotions, distorted as they are by sin, reflect something of the perfect character of God. Anger helps us understand His hatred of sin; jealousy reveals His passion for His beloved people; contempt exposes His triumphant mockery of evil. As well, fear, despair, and shame magnify the incomprehensible horror of the cross and our Lord's incarnate compassion to bear the judicial and personal consequences of our sin.

God is mysterious, but His heart and His purposes are good. In this chapter we will consider His mysterious ways of working in our lives. In the last chapter, we will focus on the goodness of His heart toward us.

THE UNPREDICTABILITY OF GOD

God is unpredictable. He will neither permit us to know our own future nor allow us to foresee when the Lord returns. There isn't any moment of life that we can look at and say: "I know what God is going to do here, and how He is going to accomplish His will." But it is possible to observe, participate, and marvel in the mystery of God.

A good friend attended one of my (Dan's) sexual abuse seminars. The material provoked a strong reaction in him, and he felt compelled to take a walk around the church parking lot. He decided to sit down on a pylon. He was struggling with the question, "Where are You, God—why don't You seem to do more for those who have been betrayed and violated?" He was also battling with loneliness. He wanted God to engage him, comfort him, and draw him into His love.

As he sat there, he noticed a small bird only a few feet away. He thought to himself with good humor and slight cynicism, "I wonder—is this bird perhaps an agent of God, sent to encourage my heart?" He recalled Dr. Doolittle talking to the animals. He thought about Elijah being nourished by the birds. He looked away.

A moment later he noticed that the bird was moving slowly toward him. To his utter astonishment, it hopped onto his hand. He was stunned. He felt oddly alive, as if he were in the presence of an act of God.

In an instant he blinked, and the bird defecated on his hand and then flew away. It left a large splotch of whitish liquid all over his hand. At that very moment, he recalled, he felt as if his other hand suddenly caught on fire. He looked at it and saw that it was covered by a mass of red ants. In pain, he began wiping away the ants with his free hand.

After knocking most of the ants off himself, he noticed that his hand was swollen, his shirt was now covered with bird excrement, and his body was wet with sweat.

He sat there on the pylon, stupefied. He had longed for God's comfort, but what he had just experienced felt like an assault of nature orchestrated by God. *What gives?* he wondered. He sat for a time and then began to laugh.

"I laughed less at the event," he later told me, "and more at the irony of how God dealt with my demands. I thought I wanted comfort. "What I really wanted, however, was not so much His comfort but His acknowledgment that I am a little boy who needs to be taken care of, not a man who has the courage to face life. Thankfully, God responded to what I deeply desire—to be respected and honored—rather than to what I thought I wanted. In an odd sense, I felt invigorated to move back into life."

Part of the mystery of God is His disruptive intrusion to provide us with what we desperately desire, not what we think we require. He does so by the use of paradox: He draws us to darkness and, in the midst of what appears awful, He shows something of His awe-full, bright goodness.

God's methods are indeed mysterious. He is the eternal artist who orchestrates horizontal circumstances to provoke us to ask hard questions about Him. And, oddly, those questions invite us to know and trust Him with a depth unavailable without asking those questions.

THE MYSTERY OF HIS METHODS

God wants us to reflect His glory, and He knows we are but dust. He knows as well that left to ourselves, we live less to reflect His splendor than to seize His glory for our own. If we are to change, we must change our orientation so that we see the path of usurping His glory as noxious and disgraceful, not as sweet and reasonable.

How does God persuade us to see the path of death as horrible and the path of life as glorious? The psalmist proclaimed, "Before I was afflicted I went astray, but now I obey your word" (Psalm 119:67). His mysterious method of persuasion is the path of pain. Affliction opens the heart to a change in direction.

Redemptive Struggle

God hurts us, and He does so intentionally. This doesn't mean that all pain comes from God—the evil one is active and destructive. It is theologically inaccurate, however, to assume that any suffering surprises or foils His purposes.

Is the death of a child a punishment from God? Not likely. Is it an assault of the evil one? Perhaps. Is it the consequence of living in a fallen, disease-ridden, accident-prone world—and not the direct, personal assault of God or the evil one? More than likely. But irrespective of causation, we can conclude that, given the sovereignty of God, all suffering is orchestrated for larger purposes.

Suffering may be caused by the hand of an enemy, but God uses sorrow for the sake of redemption. All suffering invites us to struggle with God. And the struggle with God gives us a glimpse of His character, seen in the paradox of the Cross. It is the suffering and resurrection of Christ that transforms the heart.

Listen to the cry of suffering and how it propels the psalmist to struggle with God:

How long, LORD God Almighty,
will your anger smolder
against the prayers of your people?
You have fed them with the bread of tears;
you have made them drink tears by the bowlful.
You have made us an object of derision to our neighbors,
and our enemies mock us.
Psalm 80:4-6

The psalmist has been made to eat and drink sorrow. The source of the pain is not God, but the mockery of neighbors and enemies. Yet it is God who is "behind" all suffering—shaping its form and orchestrating its direction.

The psalmist goes on to compare the people of God to a vine that God dug out of the soil of Egypt. God replanted His people in the promised land, clearing the ground and nourishing the vineyard. With all that care, the psalmist questions God: "Why have you broken down its walls so that all who pass by pick its grapes?" (Psalm 80:12). Why have You built us up and cared for us only to allow us to be broken in pieces?

Doubt, confusion, even radical struggle are required before we are inclined to surrender to His goodness. Surrender is not possible without a fight. Although we should not glorify the struggle, it is apparently provoked by God and is therefore part of the process of transformation.

We struggle with God in order to comprehend why He remains silent when we want Him to speak, why He abandons us when we want His protection, why He attacks us when we want His comfort. The mystery of His methods is that they are sometimes the opposite of what we expect. Exploring God's ways in light of the darker emotions reveals that He uses silence, abandonment, and assault to win our hearts for His glory.

The Silence of God

Listen to my prayer, O God,
> do not ignore my plea;
> hear me and answer me.
My thoughts trouble me and I am distraught
> because of what my enemy is saying,
> because of the threats of the wicked.

Psalm 55:1-3

Silence can drive us crazy. When Jesus would not answer Pilate's questions, it sent Pilate into a frenzy. Silence draws to the surface a panic to get a response. It unnerves. It traps.

A former employer of mine used to twirl his ring and look out the window as I (Dan) would present him with concerns. Many times he would look back at me with a disengaged, passing glance and then neglect to respond to my concerns. Several minutes would pass, during which he might pick up a phone and chat with someone unrelated to my pressing concerns, hang up, and then look back at me and say, "Tell me again what you want."

I wanted to plead or scream. I felt helpless. I desperately wanted something, but simultaneously I dreaded asking.

David was caught in a similar bind with God in Psalm 39. We do not know what provoked his battle with God, but we do know that he felt unnerved and trapped. He was caught between screaming at God to stop hitting him, pleading with Him to listen and not turn a deaf ear, and fleeing from God by refusing to speak:

> I said, "I will watch my ways
>   and keep my tongue from sin;
> I will put a muzzle on my mouth
>   while in the presence of the wicked."
> So I remained utterly silent,
>   not even saying anything good.
> But my anguish increased;
>   my heart grew hot within me.
> While I meditated, the fire burned;
>   then I spoke with my tongue:
> "Show me, LORD, my life's end
>   and the number of my days;
>   let me know how fleeting my life is.

You have made my days a mere handbreadth;
>   the span of my years is as nothing before you.
Everyone is but a breath,
>   even those who seem secure."

Psalm 39:1-5

David is reticent to speak. He knows that if he utters a word he is going to get into trouble, even if what he says is good. His silence, we learn later, is due to his anger toward God: "I was silent; I would not open my mouth, for you are the one who has done this" (verse 9). David was furious with God for relentlessly disciplining him.

David is trapped. If he speaks, he will be in deeper trouble. But if he doesn't speak, then his anguish will increase. The silence of God has wedged him between a rock and a hard place. His only hope is to gain perspective on the brevity and futility of life by embracing its tragedy:

Surely everyone goes around like a mere phantom;
>   in vain they rush about, heaping up wealth
>   without knowing whose it will finally be.
"But now, Lord, what do I look for?
>   My hope is in you.
Save me from all my transgressions;
>   do not make me the scorn of fools.
I was silent; I would not open my mouth,
>   for you are the one who has done this.
Remove your scourge from me;
>   I am overcome by the blow of your hand.
When you rebuke and discipline anyone for their sin,
>   you consume their wealth like a moth—
>   surely everyone is but a breath."

Psalm 39:6-11

THE CRY OF THE SOUL

David's hope is essentially found in the truth that all things, both of pain and of pleasure, pass. He sees that it is pointless to bustle around wheeling and dealing and working for more pleasure, when God can (and will) remove it in an instant.

David is irked with God, but he knows that he cannot remain silent and withdrawn from Him. Is his hope in the character of God? Is his hope the outpouring of God's mercy?

No. David's hope lies in recognizing the vanity and brevity of life. He hopes that maybe God will hear him and leave him alone for a while.

If we read this psalm as the definitive statement of David's hope, we will be misled about the nature of biblical hope. But we must come to terms with David's assessment of life as brief and painful in order to avoid misconstruing hope as something sugarcoated and cheap.

In this passage, David faces the sorrow of life head-on. He cries out for a new relationship with the One who is hurting him. He still sees God as his adversary, and he pleads with God not to deliver another blow:

> Hear my prayer, LORD,
>> listen to my cry for help;
>> be not deaf to my weeping.
> For I dwell with you as a foreigner,
>> a stranger, as all my ancestors were.
> Look away from me, that I may enjoy life again
>> before I depart and am no more.
> *Psalm 39:12-13*

David's soul cries for God to be attentive. He feels that God is deaf—particularly toward his weeping. David feels alien and cut off from God, but to whom else can he turn? He has lost the hope that withdrawal from God or wealth will alleviate his struggles.

God's silence—His refusal to respond to our plea—disrupts our confidence in the stability and safety of life and the predictability of God. It traps us. Like David, we cannot remain silent, nor can we speak easily. We can't go blithely through life assuming that most things are fine. We are caught between the silence of God and our inability to make life work.

Silence exposes our double-mindedness. David pleads with God, but in his final cry he tells God to avert His gaze. Who has not felt this way? He wants God, and he doesn't want God. "Hear me, God, but turn Your eyes away." He says in effect, "I want You to remove Your fierce hand of discipline and ignore me for a while. I will laugh and rejoice again if You simply stop intruding in my life. Go on— just leave me alone. I'll be a whole lot happier once You do. Get out of my face—why don't You?"

Silence compels struggle. God's silence forces David to wrestle honestly with God. He asks God to listen, and then he tells God to turn His face away from him. He wants God—but not if it means more suffering. Enough is enough.

The trap of silence draws out both our desire for God and our demand for relief. It exposes the internal battle between dignity and depravity. If we flee from this inner war, we also lose the voice to cry out for mercy. The apostle Paul struggled with this ambivalence, but he did not shrink back from voicing it to God:

> For in my inner being I delight in God's law; but I see
> another law at work in me, waging war against the law of
> my mind and making me a prisoner of the law of sin at
> work within me. What a wretched man I am! Who will
> rescue me from this body that is subject to death?
> *Romans 7:22-24*

Paul's cry led him to his Advocate: "Thanks be to God, who delivers me through Jesus Christ our Lord!" (Romans 7:25).

We cannot escape the quicksand of wanting and not wanting God through our own resources. So God again persuades us through the path of affliction: He allows us to feel abandoned by Him.

Abandonment by God

In addition to mourning God's silence, in other places the psalmist takes an even more brazen, irreverent, mocking attitude in response to God's apparent inattention: he calls upon God to wake up. The biblical writers knew well that God does not sleep, as did the pagan gods. The psalmist's plea for God to wake up is a furious accusation:

> Awake, Lord! Why do you sleep?
>> Rouse yourself! Do not reject us forever.
> Why do you hide your face
>> and forget our misery and oppression?
> *Psalm 44:23-24*

Sometimes it seems not merely that God is inattentive, but that He has turned away from us and forgotten us in the midst of our burdens. This is the experience of abandonment. It feels cruel. It passively allows harm to descend without offering protection. Ultimately, all abandonment feels like betrayal.

What would you feel toward a physician who walks past a bleeding accident victim in order to avoid missing the start of a movie? What would you feel toward a father who sees his daughter being sexually abused and turns away to read his paper?

What do you feel toward God when He seems to turn His face from your cries?

In language that shocks and disturbs, the psalmist tells God what it is like to feel abandoned by Him. Remember that the Psalms were not private journals, but the hymns sung during the public worship of the faithful people of God. Imagine singing these furious lyrics in your next worship service:

> You gave us up to be devoured like sheep
>   and have scattered us among the nations.
> You sold your people for a pittance,
>   gaining nothing from their sale.
> You have made us a reproach to our neighbors,
>   the scorn and derision of those around us.
> You have made us a byword among the nations;
>   the peoples shake their heads at us.
> I live in disgrace all day long,
>   and my face is covered with shame
> at the taunts of those who reproach and revile me,
>   because of the enemy, who is bent on revenge.
> All this came upon us,
>   though we had not forgotten you;
>   we had not been false to your covenant.
> Our hearts had not turned back;
>   our feet had not strayed from your path.
> But you crushed us and made us a haunt for jackals;
>   you covered us over with deep darkness.
>
> *Psalm 44:11-19*

The psalmist does something inconceivable: Enraged, he mocks God. He pours out a litany of accusations and puts God on trial for His failure to provide and protect. God has forgotten His people and left them to be devoured like helpless sheep without a shepherd. The psalmist lambastes God for foolishly selling His people and gaining nothing from their sale. He says in effect, "God is cruel; He is a fool—and His people did nothing to deserve this betrayal."

The psalmist is incredulous: God set up His own children to be decimated! This is like a father who says to a child: "Trust me: jump. I will catch you." The child jumps into midair, and the father averts his eyes and lets the child fall. The psalmist puts God on trial and finds Him guilty.

Even more incredible, God endures this accusatory attack of His people—and even blesses it as part of worship.

Step back from this thought for a moment. True, God has ordained this psalm to be part of His inspired Word and worship. But we are in dangerous waters here. Fury against God is not good. We should not glorify it as a badge of courage.

Tragically, many feel a deep sense of passion and joy in the adolescent swagger of railing against God. Fury against God can either be an unholy diatribe that glories in taking on the "big guy," or it can be a passionate, earnest cry that reveals the depths of our desperation. When it is the latter, then our expression of rage leaves us even more desperate and hungry for God.

God invites and elicits the cold fury of our soul because it is in the midst of this struggle to express our heart to Him that we enter the passion of our desire and engage in relationship with Him. It appears that He blesses passion, even when it opposes Him, as long as we move toward Him to wrestle with who He is.

The Lord honors the heart that struggles to know Him or fight Him, because He will use all human passion—for or against God— to capture our hearts for Him. Jesus indicates this in His message for the church in Laodicea: "I know your deeds, that you are neither cold nor hot. I wish you were either one or the other! So, because you are lukewarm—neither hot nor cold—I am about to spit you out of my mouth" (Revelation 3:15-16).

God desires our passion; He despises our complacency. The strong emotions that arise from abandonment deepen our hunger to know God.

Under Attack from God

It is hard enough to feel that God is silent. It is overwhelming to see God withdraw from us. But it is even worse to sense that He is attacking us:

> You have rejected us, God, and burst upon us;
>> you have been angry—now restore us!
> You have shaken the land and torn it open;
>> mend its fractures, for it is quaking.
> You have shown your people desperate times;
>> you have given us wine that makes us stagger.
>
> *Psalm 60:1-3*

The psalmist pictures God as an earthquake: breaking up land, spewing forth rock, disrupting our stability and sending us reeling. Like a drunk, we stagger under the influence of chaos.

This is a frightening image of God, but we can gain some relief from its intensity by viewing it as somewhat impersonal: An earthquake can be consigned to the category of natural disasters, rather than to the direct assault of God.

Elsewhere in the Bible, however, God reveals Himself as the one who attacks us. The image of the earthquake gives way to more violent, predatory images God. Hosea spoke of God as a beast who waits in hiding and then pounces on unsuspecting travelers, ripping them to pieces:

> I cared for you in the wilderness,
>> in the land of burning heat.
> When I fed them, they were satisfied;
>> when they were satisfied, they became proud;
>> then they forgot me.
> So I will be like a lion to them,
>> like a leopard I will lurk by the path.

Like a bear robbed of her cubs,
    I will attack them and rip them open;
like a lion I will devour them—
    a wild animal will tear them apart.

Hosea 13:5-8

We want God to be our shepherd, not a wild animal. We would prefer to defang and declaw the divine beast and domesticate His fury, but He will not allow it. The image of Christ as the Lion of Judah in Revelation (5:5) reinforces the theme of God as devouring animal.

God portrays Himself as a beast in order to make clear the depth of His ferocious love. It is a terrifying image. When did He become a beast to the people of God? It was after they rejected Him, once He had poured out blessings on them. After He fed them and they were satisfied, they became content, complacent, and proud.

God is a beast who rips away the skin of arrogance and the heart of pride. Like a responsible oncologist, He will do whatever it takes to strip us of the disease that will destroy us. He performs this surgery through the fury of others. The Psalms indicate that He will perform this surgery by using our enemies, our closest friends, natural consequences, or His own anger.[1] Irrespective of the means, however, God will not let His children wander endlessly away from Him without intervention. He will stop us cold in the midst of our prideful rebellion and compel us to seek His face.

God uses silence to unnerve us, abandonment to arouse us, and assault to stop us from pursuing idolatrous independence. He is a God of paradox. He uses darkness to deepen our desire for light. What does He want for us in using these mysterious ways of working in our lives? Even more radically, what does He want *from* us through these odd gifts of grace? It is His desire *for* and *from* us that most clearly reveals the paradox of His methods.

THE MYSTERY OF GOD'S DESIRE

A woman who had suffered a great deal asked one day, "What does God want from me?" Then her eyes suddenly widened. She leaned forward and said: "Is it possible? Did I just say: 'What does He want from me?'" Although she had been a believer for more than two decades, it was the first moment in her life that she considered the possibility that God wanted something from her. He did not merely want something *for* her, such as being a good wife, a loving mother, or a faithful worker in her church; He actually wanted something *from* her.

The mystery of God's desire for us is revealed in His pain. Listen to the cry of God:

> Listen, my people, and I will speak;
>> I will testify against you, Israel:
>> I am God, your God.
> I bring no charges against you concerning your sacrifices
>> or concerning your burnt offerings, which are ever before me.
> I have no need of a bull from your stall
>> or of goats from your pens,
> for every animal of the forest is mine,
>> and the cattle on a thousand hills.
> I know every bird in the mountains,
>> and the insects in the fields are mine.
> If I were hungry I would not tell you,
>> for the world is mine, and all that is in it.
> Do I eat the flesh of bulls
>> or drink the blood of goats?
> Sacrifice thank offerings to God,
>> fulfill your vows to the Most High,
> and call on me in the day of trouble;
>> I will deliver you, and you will honor me.
>
> *Psalm 50:7-15*

God feels the anguish of being misunderstood and ignored. He responds with anger, sarcasm, and longing. He rebukes His people not because of their failure of obedience; they had fulfilled the letter of the law and brought Him a legion of burnt offerings. He was angry because His children misunderstood His desire for their heart.

And so God redemptively mocks His people, asking, "Do you think I am hungry for meat, or thirsty for blood?" After anger and sarcasm, He lays out His desire: "I want your gratitude, your loyalty, and your passion. I want your heart."

David had a grasp of God's desire:

You do not delight in sacrifice, or I would bring it;
    you do not take pleasure in burnt offerings.
My sacrifice, O God, is a broken spirit;
    a broken and contrite heart
    you, God, will not despise.
Psalm 51:16-17

Tragically, we often believe God wants flesh and blood. We think of Him as did the older brother in the story of the prodigal son:

The older brother became angry and refused to go in. So
his father went out and pleaded with him. But he answered
his father, "Look! All these years I've been slaving for you
and never disobeyed your orders. Yet you never gave me
even a young goat so I could celebrate with my friends. But
when this son of yours who has squandered your property
with prostitutes comes home, you kill the fattened calf
for him!"

"My son," the father said, "you are always with me, and
everything I have is yours. But we had to celebrate and be

glad, because this brother of yours was dead and is alive
again; he was lost and is found."
Luke 15:28-32

The older brother viewed God as a slavemaster, a hard man who took no delight in him or in the desires of his heart. This brother labored for his father in the way we often do for God: by rote, soullessly obedient—not with the sensual passion and full-blooded engagement of joining a party to celebrate the wonder of our reconciliation with God.

God wants us to adore Him, dance with Him, eat, drink, and sing with Him in the experience of His awesome, glorious love. The mystery of His desire is that an eternal, infinite, holy, and utterly self-fulfilling Being wants us—and He is willing to go to any lengths whatsoever to disrupt, arouse, and stop us from pursuing any lover other than Himself. He is willing to go to the extreme of bearing our anger—and even more, pouring out His anger on His beloved Son, Being of His own Being. Through His unfathomable desire for us and His paradoxical methods of wooing us, He reveals His goodness. As we will see in the next chapter, His goodness invites us to a privilege that is beyond words.

17

The Goodness of God

God encounters us in surprising ways. He is mysterious, and His intrusions into our lives are unpredictable.

At first, it is thrilling to realize that God cares enough to draw us closer to Himself. And it is exciting to think that He often chooses to meet us when we least expect it. But if we're honest, the thought of a disruptive and intrusive God also frightens and even repels us. We would prefer Him to be manageable and predictable. It is precisely at this point that we need to understand the infinite goodness of God.

My (Tremper's) middle son, at this stage of his life, loves two activities: video games and reading. Most people would agree that, unless he grows up to be a fighter pilot, the latter is better for his development than the former, but even his reading gets out of hand. Night after night my wife and I have to browbeat the boy to stop reading and go to sleep. On occasion, I even have to sneak up behind him while he is deeply absorbed and grab the book out of his hands.

Timmy would prefer to read all night—and he would, if we weren't there to stop him. On occasions when Alice and I have fallen asleep before settling him down for the night, he has stayed up half the night reading until he finishes a book. The next day he is too tired and ornery to do anything until he gets into bed that next night and, forgetting his exhaustion, starts reading. The cycle begins again.

Tim needs to be disrupted for his own good, even if it's done against his will, because left to his natural desires he would burn himself out. We have to be tough with him. At the point of disruption, he often sees me as an enemy, not a loving parent.

The analogy is not perfect, but God, too, confronts us at times in unpredictable, unwanted, and painful ways. At the point of heartache, we do not naturally view Him as our friend and loving parent. Our deepest questions about Him arise in the context of physical pain, shattered dreams, and disappointed desire—*God, are You good? Are You real? Do You exist?*

God isn't unnecessarily cruel; He does not enjoy our pain. When God encounters us with loneliness, silence, and struggle, He does so because He has an unimaginable pleasure for us: *In our suffering He reveals His goodness.* He wants us to revel in His glorious love. And it is in the midst of darkness that the brightness of His loves shines with startling intensity. It is almost as if the darkness serves as a frame to focus our eyes on the centrality of His desire—pictured in the image of the Cross.

THE YEARNING OF GOD

God desires us; that truth alone is incomprehensible. But what He wants is staggering—He does not want robotic obedience, but passionate engagement.

The book of Hosea presents us with a picture of a God whose heart burns for His rebellious people. The Israelites reject Him, but

God is unwilling either to discard them or to back off. He persists in His desire to be their God.

Hosea's ministry, in the mid-eighth century BC, stands out against a background of widespread indifference and hostility toward God. This was an unusual period in Israelite history. Normally, Israel struggled in squeeze plays between superpowers on both north and south. But at this point in Israel's history, those powers—located in Egypt and Mesopotamia—were weak, allowing Israel to expand and prosper.

We know from experience the pitfalls of power and privilege. Prosperity—a day of ease—often leads to disregard for God, which in turn leads to relational decay. Hosea's day was characterized by oppression and self-interest. Much of Hosea's prophecy portrays God's anger toward Israel because of their rebellion toward Him.

The images Hosea uses to describe God are particularly vivid in revealing God's attitude toward His rebellious people. Hosea likens God's anger toward Israel to the anger of a husband who has just discovered that his wife has been selling herself to other men.[1] Israel, God's bride, is a whore, and God reacts with intense jealousy. In another passage (5:12) God likens Himself to a moth and to rot: He irritates and subtly damages His people as a moth eats holes in clothing or rot ruins food.

Further, God's anger also takes the form of frontal attack. He is a ferocious lion who will rip His people into bloody strips (5:14). God, the Maker of creation, will use all of creation—whether the subtle intrusion of an irritating insect or the fearful pounce of a wild beast—to win back His most precious creation: humankind.

Because the Israelites are wandering down dangerous paths, God confronts them in painful ways. They will suffer. His coming judgment toward them is also given metaphorical expression: for instance, God will forcibly yoke Israel, the recalcitrant heifer (10:11). The people and their earthly king are like debris floating on water: helpless, they will simply be carried away into oblivion (10:7).

223

Historically, Hosea was anticipating the coming destruction of Israel in 722 BC, when the ruthless Assyrian army would sweep down from the north to carry off the ten northern tribes and hover over the two southern tribes (known as Judah) to keep them in line. In this way God confronted His people and made them suffer. But their suffering would be for a purpose. Hosea relates to us God's own words:

How can I give you up, Ephraim?
    How can I hand you over, Israel?
How can I treat you like Admah?
    How can I make you like Zeboyim?
My heart is changed within me;
    all my compassion is aroused.
I will not carry out my fierce anger,
    nor will I devastate Ephraim again.
For I am God, and not a man—
    the Holy One among you.
    I will not come against their cities.

Hosea 11:8-9

God did not completely destroy the northern kingdom (here called Ephraim/Israel), though they deserved it for turning against Him and oppressing the helpless and poor. Instead of depicting the end of His people, this passage describes His incredible love for them even while they were slapping Him in the face.

At pivotal points in his prophecy, Hosea uses still more images to highlight God's redemptive purpose. The Lord is a forgiving husband to Israel (3:1-5): Though His promiscuous wife repeatedly sins against Him, He continually allows her to come back to Him. The Lord is a healing physician (6:1-2): Though He afflicts His people in judgment, He also binds their wounds. The Lord is a lion (11:10):

Though He rends His people in judgment, He also ferociously protects the faithful remnant. These and many other startling images of divine compassion and restoration permeate the book.

GOD'S CHANGE OF HEART

Hosea indicates that God had decided to obliterate His people but then changed His mind. He remains tenaciously committed to them: He neither destroys them nor allows them to live as they please—because He knows that they would be miserable and ultimately destroy themselves.

God changed His mind. These words should send shock waves through us. Through Moses, He had warned His people long ago that if they sinned He would destroy them. They fully deserved it; there was no question about their guilt. But God couldn't bring Himself to do it. His purity demanded the eradication of all that was contrary to His character, but His mercy cried out to restore His beloved children.

It appears that God was in conflict with Himself here. What are we to do with such a picture? The history of interpretation has often consigned this depiction to mere metaphor: God has no actual feelings, and even if He did a perfect being certainly could not feel conflict. But the text is unequivocal: God changed His mind in the midst of an internal conflict. Frankly, more staggering than that—He changed it in our favor.

Some might protest that Hosea's portrayal simply casts God in the image of fickle humanity. However, note how God justifies His change of heart: "I am God, and not a man" (11:9). It is precisely because He *is* God that He changes His mind. Place a human being in the middle of such internal ambivalence, and if he had the power and the ability to get away with it, we could expect that he would simply get rid of the person who caused the conflict. But God harbors divine compassion for His people.

Jesus incarnates in human form the passion that God feels toward His people. Jesus went to the extreme of suffering with us and for us. He felt our loneliness, our fears, our shame, our anger. God's intense desire for relationship with His people led to the Cross: "For God so loved the world that he gave his one and only Son, that whoever believes in him shall not perish but have eternal life" (John 3:16).

God confronts us with pain and suffering because He desires to reveal His goodness to us. But the goodness of God will not be validated by any attempt to prove it apart from faith. We experience His goodness only through the revelation of His glory. And the supreme picture of His glory can be seen only through the irony of the Cross. Through this irony, God compels us to look at Him with wide-eyed wonder.

THE IRONY OF GOD'S GOODNESS

As we experience the pain—anger, fear, jealousy, despair, contempt, and shame—of the fallen world, we may come to question God's goodness.

We have seen, however, that God works in mysterious ways, revealing Himself to us in the midst of the world's pain. Indeed, God reveals Himself as supremely good in the heart of the most intense evil and suffering experienced on earth. This is the irony of the Cross.

Jesus was nailed to the cross by people whose only intention was to kill Him and thus get Him out of the way. But the suffering they intended for evil was divinely transformed to the goodness of salvation and freedom from guilt:

Fellow Israelites, listen to this: Jesus of Nazareth was a man accredited by God to you by miracles, wonders and signs, which God did among you through him, as you yourselves know. This man was handed over to you by God's deliberate

plan and foreknowledge; and you, with the help of wicked
men, put him to death by nailing him to the cross. But
God raised him from the dead, freeing him from the agony
of death, because it was impossible for death to keep its
hold on him.

Acts 2:22-24

The first irony of the Cross is that *evil intention is transformed into divine salvation*. God overruled the wicked intention of those who wanted Jesus dead and used their very act to bring salvation to the world.

The second irony of the Cross is that *resurrection comes through crucifixion*. This irony is heightened when we see that the Bible understands the Cross to be the culmination of a great cosmic battle. The events in Genesis initiate the battle when Adam and Eve sin at Satan's instigation. In the midst of the consequent alienation and curse, God gives Adam and Eve a word of hope: They will not be turned over to the powers of evil, but a conflict will rage between God and His people on the one hand, and Satan and his followers on the other.

The rest of the Bible comprises the struggle between God's people and Satan's followers (or, as Augustine put it, "the city of God and the city of man"). The climax occurs in the Gospels, when Jesus confronts Satan and demonstrates His power over the demonic realm in numerous encounters. But as Paul explains, it is on the cross that Jesus once and for all defeats Satan:

When you were dead in your sins and in the uncircumcision
of your flesh, God made you alive with Christ. He forgave
us all our sins, having canceled the charge of our legal
indebtedness, which stood against us and condemned us;
he has taken it away, nailing it to the cross. And having

disarmed the powers and authorities, he made a public
spectacle of them, triumphing over them by the cross.
Colossians 2:13-15

Paul describes the crucifixion as a great military victory over the
demonic realm ("the powers and authorities"). The ultimate victory is won not by killing, but by dying. The Suffering Servant has
become the Victorious Savior.

God overturns pain by experiencing it. He displays His goodness
by suffering on our behalf. His suffering does not free His people
from the pain of the fallen world; indeed, we are privileged to share
Christ's suffering during our lives. In essence, Christ's victory invests
our present pain with significance and gives us a sure hope that we
will move from suffering to glory.[2]

FROM SUFFERING TO GLORY

We cautioned earlier against assuming we can directly alter our emotions. It has not been our goal to provide a guide for conquering
unwanted emotions. Efforts to "change" troubling emotions often
involve an effort to "master" God through attempts to escape the
heartache of the Fall.

The goal of avoiding heartache is both impossible and undesirable. It is impossible because we live in a fallen world and are fun-
damentally flawed beings—as Genesis 3, one of the foundational
passages of the Bible, teaches. Perfection is reserved for heaven; while
we live, we will be both the vehicles and the recipients of unrighteous
emotions. This is not a warrant to justify our internal ugliness, but
it clears the air of any overly optimistic assessment of human ability.

The goal to evade anguish is undesirable because our dark emotions have a redemptive side (although this fact does not make them
any less painful). Though tainted in our expression of them, they

nonetheless reflect the character of God. They have the power to vocalize our deepest cry—and when that cry is uttered before God, our hearts are exposed and transformed as we glimpse His heart for us.

Nowhere does the Bible promise that our earthly lives will be untouched by suffering. Just the contrary, in fact: the New Testament repeatedly warns that pain and suffering are part and parcel of the Christian life. But that is not bad news; it is the gospel ("good news"), for it is through our pain and suffering that we experience joy and encounter glory:

> Now if we are children, then we are heirs—heirs of God and co-heirs with Christ, if indeed we share in his sufferings in order that we may also share in his glory.
>
> *Romans 8:17*

> [And] we boast in the hope of the glory of God. Not only so, but we also glory in our sufferings, because we know that suffering produces perseverance; perseverance, character; and character, hope. And hope does not put us to shame, because God's love has been poured out into our hearts through the Holy Spirit, who has been given to us.
>
> *Romans 5:2-5*

Paradoxically, God reveals Himself in our suffering. There is no resurrection without crucifixion; no glory without suffering. Healing, therefore, isn't quite what we thought it would be. Our dark emotions reveal God; they open the road to true joy. This is the central message of the book of Psalms: *We encounter divine goodness in the midst of pain.*

Our focus in this book has required us to concentrate on one particular type of psalm, the lament. As model prayers for the Israelites to approach God in worship, the laments offered a voice to articulate suffering. They express all the difficult emotions we experience today—anger, fear, jealousy, despair, shame, and contempt. Crucially important, however, is the fact that in the end the laments turn to joy, comfort, trust, and worship. In other words, they turn to God. This is where suffering drives us.

The transition from suffering to glory in the lament psalms is always abrupt, mysterious, unexpected. Psalm 69 provides a good example.

Psalm 69: From Pleading to Praise

David begins the psalm with a cry to God to save him from his troubles. These troubles are unspecified, but they are painted in vivid images. He describes his life and his feelings as similar to being stuck in the middle of a river with the water up to his neck. He is about to drown, and there is nothing he can do about it. Throughout the psalm he complains about his enemies and expresses his fears and anger. He concludes his complaint with a brief, hard-hitting self-description: "afflicted and in pain" (verse 29).

It is just this suffering, however, that drives David to call on God in the first place. He needs God to protect him because he can't do it, nor is anyone else willing or able to help. Precisely because his vision moves from his suffering to God, there is an incredibly abrupt change of mood at the end—typical of virtually all laments in the Psalms—from pain to joy:

> I will praise God's name in song
>   and glorify him with thanksgiving.
> This will please the LORD more than an ox,
>   more than a bull with its horns and hooves.
> The poor will see and be glad—
>   you who seek God, may your hearts live!

THE GOODNESS OF GOD

The LORD hears the needy
    and does not despise his captive people.
Let heaven and earth praise him,
    the seas and all that move in them,
for God will save Zion
    and rebuild the cities of Judah.
Then people will settle there and possess it;
    the children of his servants will inherit it,
    and those who love his name will dwell there.

Psalm 69:30-36

The abruptness of the emotional transition in this and other lament psalms suggests a mistaken impression that the psalmist almost magically changed his mood. This reading does not take into account the fact that the psalm has compressed an experience that took a long time to develop into a short statement.

Still, the transition is mysterious. The psalms provide no formula for the bridge from lament to joy— no steps to healing, no principles to practice. God does not tolerate manipulation of truth to escape from struggle. He longs for faith that struggles and rests in His goodness.

This is not to say that we are without biblical principles for living with our emotions and seeking changed hearts. But all such principles—for example, "a gentle answer turns away wrath"—are conditional upon the direction of our hearts. Attempting to use God for magical applications of truth to conjure a new reality is radically different from seeking to live out His glorious character.

If we could explain the gap in Psalm 69 between verses 29 and 30, then we could control it. But that would violate God's character as the One who rescues us from our troubles. The only thing we know for sure about the transition from suffering to glory is that God is the One who effects it—although He may choose any number of surprising ways to minister to our hurting souls. Thus the psalmist's only recourse is to appeal to God for help and wait with confidence that He will turn sorrow into joy:

> Restore our fortunes, LORD,
>   like streams in the Negev.
> Those who sow with tears
>   will reap with songs of joy.
> Those who go out weeping,
>   carrying seed to sow,
> will return with songs of joy,
>   carrying sheaves with them.
> *Psalm 126:4-6*

The psalmist hungers and thirsts for God. He calls out to the Lord to satisfy His people's cravings. He looks to the Lord to provide abundant water in a dry wilderness. He anticipates abundant harvests of life-giving grain. In this way, the psalm charts a progression from suffering to goodness, from the experience of grief to joy.

What is the character of God's goodness? What is the nature of the joy He provides?

THE NATURE OF GOD'S GOODNESS

Christianity affirms the goodness of God and the reality of joy in the Christian life. But all too often these truths are misrepresented in popular understanding.

Most dangerous is the belief that Christians can experience a joy untouched by the suffering of the world, which simply transcends the anger, fear, jealousy, despair, shame, and contempt of everyday life. It is sometimes expressed in the statement, "Our heart is in heaven and not on the earth!"

THE GOODNESS OF GOD

This attitude often accompanies the idea that God's goodness is defined primarily or exclusively in terms of material prosperity, success, and good health. God loves His people and is able to give them anything they want, so Christians should look optimistically to the future for the fulfillment of their desires.

It is true that God often does give His people many good earthly gifts and instills within their hearts an almost ecstatic joy. But it is wrong to believe that all of us can expect to be recipients of this type of divine goodness and experience heavenly joy on earth continuously throughout our lives.

Human experience alone fails to support this position. No matter how much faith we have, no matter how much good we do, no matter how much effort we invest, we cannot make the difficulties and tragedies of life go away.

Beyond human experience, however, we have the authority of the Scriptures as a correcting voice for this misunderstanding of divine goodness and human joy. As the Psalms so poignantly testify, God's people do suffer. They are well acquainted with life's agonizing difficulties.

Generally, most believers do not take these distorted understandings to extremes. They realize that the Bible does not teach a "health and wealth" gospel. They know that pain and suffering will be part of their lives. But they also have some pretty clear ideas of how suffering should operate in their lives.

The assumptions about God's methods for using suffering usually center on three conditions: To be fruitful, the suffering should be: (1) temporary, (2) understandable, and (3) readily applicable to life's practical realities.

First, God may need to use suffering to get me back on the right track, but it only needs to be a quick jolt to get the message across. Therefore my experience of suffering should be to the point, nothing chronic.

Second, in order for the message behind the suffering to be clear, the experience must be understandable. To profit from it, therefore, I must be able to explain it. "God allowed this to happen in my life because . . ."

Finally, the clarity of the suffering must lead to ready application. If I know what the lessons are and how to apply them to the way I live, I need not go through the pain again.

Unfortunately, these views of suffering are too neat: They don't conform to experience. That leaves many people spending most of their lives in frustrated attempts to identify the specific reasons for their pain.

To understand the true nature of the goodness and joy we encounter in the midst of suffering, we can turn once again to the Psalms for guidance. Here we see God's goodness, which leads to joy, described as a series of actions that He does for us. This subject could fill an entire book, but we will sample a taste of God's bounty for us by noting a few of the many ways He expresses His love for His hurting people.

THE EXPRESSIONS OF GOD'S GOODNESS

In the midst of daily struggles, we hunger and hope. Deep inside we know that life is not all it was meant to be—we were built for something better. What is it that we crave? What is it that we expect both in this life and in the life to come?

It is impossible to answer these questions meaningfully within ourselves. We have already seen that the Psalms voice the cry of our souls; it should not be surprising that they also voice the hunger and hope of our souls.

God Restores Us

The LORD is my shepherd, I lack nothing.
He makes me lie down in green pastures,

he leads me beside quiet waters,
  he refreshes my soul.
Psalm 23: 1-3

The LORD is close to the brokenhearted
  and saves those who are crushed in spirit.
Psalm 34:18

He raises the poor from the dust
  and lifts the needy from the ash heap;
he seats them with princes,
  with the princes of his people.
He settles the childless woman in her home
  as a happy mother of children.
Psalm 113:7-9

We are broken people. We face the spilled blood of Cain's hatred each day of our lives. In honest moments, we smell the charred remains of lost dreams and broken promises. The Psalms acknowledge that as God's people we are a community of sufferers, burdened by our own failings as well as the attack and abandonment of others.

Our hunger is to escape from such brokenness, and this craving gives birth to hope. It is first a hope that our sins have been forgiven, that the deepest wounds in our souls have been healed. As we experience that healing, we gain confidence that someday all our brokenness will be healed.

The psalmists attest that our God is a God who restores. They proclaim that God intervenes in the lives of His hurting people and ministers to them. He restores them when they are weak and in pain. He heals them and restores their strength. He reverses their fortunes from nothing to great glory.

Therefore, we are called to imagine what God has prepared for us in the future—perfection, glory, utter restoration. We are called to let our hearts swell with a passion to live out restoration by seeking to redress injustice, create beauty, and rest in the moments of restored relationship that point toward the day of perfect healing.

God Parents Us

> A father to the fatherless, a defender of widows,
>   is God in his holy dwelling.
> *Psalm 68:5*

> As a father has compassion on his children,
>   so the LORD has compassion on those who fear him.
> *Psalm 103:13*

We are a lonely and frightened people, in need of protection and nourishment. We know we are defenseless against harm. We long for someone bigger and stronger to stand between us and all hurt; we crave someone who is better and kinder to nurture our heart.

The Psalms describe God as our Parent. He cares for us like a Father—but one vastly superior to any human parent. Even the best father makes mistakes and is unable to do everything he would like to do to raise, protect, and provide for his child. God, however, is able to love His children more absolutely. Where a human parent lacks resources, God gives Himself as our resource. Where a human parent lacks time, God transcends time. Where a human parent lacks interest, God faithfully pursues His people.

Our present hope, therefore, in the language of the New Testament, is that God will adopt us—for when He does, He promises us an inheritance, which includes being with Him for eternity in heaven. Therefore, we are to embrace our hunger to be in a family. No matter what our experiences have been with earthly parents or as parents to our children, we are to give voice to the cry within us for the Father who nourishes us and protects us.

THE GOODNESS OF GOD

God Gives Us Rest

> Return to your rest, my soul,
>> for the LORD has been good to you.
>
> *Psalm 116:7*

> My heart is not proud, LORD,
>> my eyes are not haughty;
> I do not concern myself with great matters
>> or things too wonderful for me.
> But I have calmed and quieted myself,
>> I am like a weaned child with its mother;
>> like a weaned child I am content.
>
> *Psalm 131:1-2*

We live in a hectic world. We seem to spend our lives rushing from one task to another. If we take a break from the furor of the world, it seems that only more labor awaits us when we jump back into the fray. In fact, any pause just increases the frenzied insanity around us. The work is never done.

This predicament is the dark consequence of the curse in Eden. We hunger for relief from it. We keep our shoulder to the wheel of life, but we yearn for even a momentary cessation that does not increase the workload once we return.

Psalm 131 demonstrates that any rest, any Sabbath, in the present life is a gift of relaxing in the humility of our finiteness. We are able to taste a moment of eternal rest when we refuse to exult in the self-importance of our tasks.

The image of mother and child in Psalm 131 reveals that God is the cause behind the psalmist's rest. The weaned child and its mother is analogous to the psalmist's soul and God. The psalmist rests in God as the child rests in a mother's arms.

Stillness is a great gift of God in the midst of a frenzied world. The promise of an eternity of Sabbath is to be lived out each day, each week. It is a rest that laughs at the intolerant demands of pressing crises with the quiet, weaned confidence that our bellies will one day be filled with the sweet milk of God.

God Fills Us

The poor will eat and be satisfied;
>they who seek the LORD will praise him—
>may your hearts live forever!
Psalm 22:26

For he satisfies the thirsty
>and fills the hungry with good things.
Psalm 107:9

He upholds the cause of the oppressed
>and gives food to the hungry.
The LORD sets prisoners free,
>the LORD gives sight to the blind,
the LORD lifts up those who are bowed down,
>the LORD loves the righteous.
The LORD watches over the foreigner
>and sustains the fatherless and the widow,
>but he frustrates the ways of the wicked.
Psalm 146:7-9

In many ways, we are empty people. We live to be filled with food, drink, companionship, contentment. And this side of paradise, we never are completely satisfied.

The psalmist tells us, however, that we do get a taste of what is to come—an hors d'oeuvre to the final banquet. We learn that both the preview and the eternal feast are gifts from a gracious God.

Therefore, the psalmist urges us to live with hunger. Refuse to demean the emptiness of the heart by trying to fill it or flee from it. Succumb to neither pious happiness nor cynical disillusionment. Taste hunger as the pang of anticipation that arouses the heart to savor the meal that awaits. Relish every good morsel of His grace—in a delicious dinner, in a well-crafted song, in a hilarious joke, in all the other tastes of the wedding banquet. Let even the prayer over your nightly meal be as much a cry as a grateful thanks for the taste of what is to come.

God Glorifies Us

But you, LORD, are a shield around me,
　　my glory, the One who lifts my head high.
Psalm 3:3

You make your saving help my shield,
　　and your right hand sustains me;
　　your help has made me great.
Psalm 18:35

What is mankind that you are mindful of them,
　　human beings that you care for them?
You have made them a little lower than the angels
　　and crowned them with glory and honor.
You made them rulers over the works of your hands;
　　you put everything under their feet:
all flocks and herds,
　　and the animals of the wild,
the birds in the sky,
　　and the fish in the sea,
　　all that swim the paths of the seas.
Psalm 8:4-8

We live in a world that oppresses us by treating us as worthless or inconsequential. We are one of millions, even billions—a grain of sand on a vast seashore, indistinguishable from the mass of humanity.

We desire more than feeling lost in the sea of existence. We want to be recognized; we want someone to stand up and take notice of us as a unique individual. And not just for fifteen minutes of fame; we want to join God in a glory that startles even the heavenly host.

Once again, only God can satisfy this hunger. The good news of the Psalms is that the Almighty God of the universe not only knows we exist, He glorifies us. He stoops down to lift us up to the glory in which we were meant to be clothed.

Psalm 8 contains one of the most startling passages in the Bible: We are made a little lower than God. The translations of the Hebrew invariably turn away from the staggering comparison by using phrases such as "gods" or "heavenly beings" or "angels." This is not what the original passage says. It contends that our glory—even corrupted by sin—*is just a little lower than God.* This is not merely an exaltation of humanity; it is a revelation of God's passion to make us like Himself.

From the beginning of time, as the creation accounts tell us and the psalmist reminds us, God intended men and women for greatness. Humanity is the apex of His creation. Even as fallen creatures, the human race can still be called glorious. How much more when we are drawn into God's presence in heaven? Therefore, we cannot imagine what we will be; how we will look; how we will feel. All we can know is that it will be a wonder that will transform every moment of shame, loss, and pain in the light of the glory that will be revealed.

God Gives Us Himself

For the LORD is righteous,
    he loves justice;
      the upright will see his face.
Psalm 11:7

As for me, I will be vindicated and will see your face;
　　when I awake, I will be satisfied with seeing your likeness.
Psalm 17:15

We hunger for God. Augustine recognized this, observing that those who did not believe were characterized by a restlessness for something greater, for something divine. The writer of Ecclesiastes declares that God "has also set eternity in the human heart" (3:11).

The Psalms voice our hope for God's ultimate good gift: Himself. He grants us fellowship with Him. We experience this hope now in the person of Jesus Christ, who "made his dwelling among us" (John 1:14). But this, too, is just an anticipation of what is to come. We look ahead as we rejoice in the One who has said "Yes, I am corning soon" (Revelation 22:20).

What, then, is the character of God's goodness? In the midst of a fallen world, created good by God but plunged into darkness by human sin, God nonetheless satisfies our hunger and gives us hope. Our joy springs from these divine gifts. It is a joy in the midst of suffering because we know that the core of this goodness can never be removed from us—that core is God Himself.

This joy is not a superficial response that ignores the problems in our lives, but a profound emotion that is confident in facing the darkness with open eyes. It is a joy that issues in thanksgiving and praise: a joy that leads to worship.

FROM LAMENT TO GRATITUDE TO WORSHIP

The revelation of God's goodness in the midst of our suffering leads us to service and worship. In a sinful world, we are surprised by His concern; we are amazed at His grace.

The laments of the Psalms begin with our internal world. They

241

articulate our dark emotions, give voice to the cry of our souls. But ultimately, they drive us to God.

What is true for the individual lament, as it moves from petition and complaint to praise and joy, is also true for the relationship between the lament and the two other major types of psalms in the Psalter—the thanksgiving song and the hymn of praise. These three genres are integrally related to one another. One leads to another, beginning with the lament.

The lament song complains to God of present trouble and calls on God to intervene. Once God answers that prayer, the worshiper turns to the thanksgiving songs, in which he utters thanks to God for hearing and answering his prayer—often quoting his previous requests in the context of thanking God for answering them. The thanksgiving song leads to the third type—the hymn of unalloyed praise to God.[3]

These three form a triad: the lament leading to the thanksgiving song and culminating in the hymn. The first is the voice of one who feels out of relationship with God, angry with God, afraid of God. The second is sung in the voice of astonished gratitude: The relationship has been reconciled. The third is sung in a voice of joy for continued fellowship with God; the worshiper feels no obstacles in his relationship with God. Walter Brueggemann has helpfully described these three as psalms of disorientation, psalms of reorientation, and psalms of orientation. There are indeed psalms for every season of life.

It is crucial for us to remember that although the Psalms begin with our internal world, they don't allow us to dwell there, fixated on our problems and dark emotions. Although they express and minister to our emotional lives, they are not a psychology text. The Psalter is a book of worship, driving us to God by insisting that we look to Him in the midst of our pain. When we do so, we find ourselves and our problems absorbed into His bright glory.

THE CALL TO PILGRIMAGE

The psalmists knew their origins from the book of Genesis. They traced their national and religious heritage back to Abraham, the father of the Hebrew faith.

God had called Abraham out of Ur, a prosperous Mesopotamian city, and commanded him to go to Canaan. It was a call to leave stability, habit, and security for wandering on a journey to a promised land. Once he got there, his wandering did not cease. He moved continually from the fringe of one city to another, never living long in one area.

In one sense, the land was his and his descendants', but in another it wasn't. Abraham was called to a life of pilgrimage as a stranger and alien in a foreign land. It was a life filled with struggles, characterized by desire and hope for the fulfillment of the divine promise of descendants and a home.

The psalmists were Abraham's biological and spiritual descendants. Those who wrote the psalms and the worshipers who used them were settled in the land of Canaan, but they knew that this was not the end of the battle. They still faced the struggles of those who wander. Their poetic compositions expressed their continuing troubles, desires, and hopes. As inspired Scripture, they were a divine gift to give voice to the torments and aspirations of God's people.

Like Abraham and the psalmists, we too are pilgrims—wanderers in a foreign land, looking ahead to the end of our journey. Our homecoming will take place in heaven as our Father greets us with open arms. Until then, we too struggle, desire, and hope.

The Psalter invites us to feel emotion without immediate resolution. It not only permits dark emotions; it demands that we be overwhelmed by what we cannot control or change. Oddly, it is in our helplessness to change what unnerves us, in our cry of desperation, that we hear the song of eternity coursing through us even when we are deaf to hope.

Listen: it grows. The music comes when it is least expected, least deserved, least understood. It is the faint sound that allures us to continue on the journey awaiting the ovation, the rousing applause of heaven.

NOTES

INTRODUCTION

1. For a comprehensive overview of how to interpret the Psalms, see Tremper Longman III, *How to Read the Psalms* (Downers Grove, IL: InterVarsity Press, 1988).

CHAPTER TWO—THE PSALMS: THE VOICE OF THE SOUL

1. John Calvin, *Institutes of the Christian Religion*, Beveridge, trans. (Grand Rapids, MI: Eerdmans, 1986), section.
2. John Calvin, *Psalms* (Grand Rapids, MI: Baker, 1981 reprint; 1571), xxxvii.
3. Walter Brueggemann, *Old Testament Theology: Essays on Structure, Theme, and Text* (Minneapolis, MN: Fortress, 1992), 29.

CHAPTER SEVEN—CONSTRUCTIVE FEAR: THE FEAR OF THE LORD

1. C. S. Lewis, *The Lion, the Witch and the Wardrobe* (New York: Macmillan, 1950), 64.

CHAPTER NINE—DIVINE DESIRE: THE JEALOUS LOVE OF GOD

1. On the warning against envy, see Proverbs 3:31; 14:30; 23:17; and 24:1. On the teaching of envy as an ugly human emotion, see Ecclesiastes 4:4; Romans 1:29; 1 Corinthians 13:4; Galatians 5:21; and James 3:14, 16. On envy as motivation for Jesus' arrest, see Matthew 27:18.
2. On the image of God spreading his blanket for love, see Ezekiel 16. On God luring his bride into the desert for love, see Hosea 2. For a portrayal of Jesus as the Bridegroom, see Revelation 19:6-9.

CHAPTER ELEVEN—REDEMPTIVE DESPAIR: THE RESTORATION OF HOPE

1. See Hebrews 2:18 and 4:15.
2. See Matthew 27:46.
3. H. N. Ridderbos, *Matthew* (Grand Rapids, MI: Zondervan, 1975), 532.

CHAPTER TWELVE—UNHOLY CONTEMPT: EVIL'S MOCKERY

1. See Romans 1:29 and 2 Corinthians 12:20.
2. On arrogant boasting about power, see Exodus 15:9. About desires, see Psalm 10:3; James 3:14; and 1 John 2:16. About wealth, see Psalm 49:6. About cleverness, see Proverbs 20:14. About the future, see Proverbs 27:1. About abilities, see Isaiah 10:15; Jeremiah 9:23-24; and 1 Corinthians 4:7.

CHAPTER FOURTEEN—THE CORROSIVE POWER OF HUMAN SHAME

1. Jeff VanVonderen, *Tired of Trying to Measure Up* (Minneapolis, MN: Bethany House Publishers, 1989), 41.
2. John Bradshaw, *Healing the Shame That Binds You* (Deerfield Beach, IL: Health Communications, 1988), vii.

CHAPTER FIFTEEN—THE REDEEMING POWER OF DIVINE SHAME

1. L. Berkhof, *Systematic Theology* (Grand Rapids, MI: Eerdmans, 1939), 339.
2. See Jeremiah 3:3; 6:15; 8:12; Zephaniah 3:5; Philippians 3:18-19.

CHAPTER SIXTEEN—THE MYSTERY OF GOD

1. On God's use of enemies to draw us to himself, see Psalm 80:5-7; of our closest friends, see Psalm 55:12-14 and 88:8; of natural consequences, see Psalm 81:12; of his own anger, see Psalm 60:1 and 74:1.

CHAPTER SEVENTEEN—THE GOODNESS OF GOD

1. See chapters 1–3 and especially 2:2-13.
2. See 2 Corinthians 1:5; Romans 8:17-18; Philippians 3:10; and 1 Peter 4:13.
3. For examples of thanksgiving songs, see Psalm 18 and 30. On the psalmist's tendency to quote previous requests in the context of thanksgiving, see Psalm 30:8-10. For an example of the hymn of praise, see Psalm 29.

ACKNOWLEDGMENTS

"'The test of all happiness is gratitude,' said G. K. Chesterton. Happy is the man who is yoked with good friends to a task that exposes the worst we can be and draws out the best we are meant to offer. He will be grateful even in the midst of assault, loneliness, and heartache."

This was the opening paragraph of the acknowledgments in the first edition of this book. What then followed was naming a set of friends that were involved in my life at the time of writing. I included musicians I was strengthened by as I wrote. I thanked our keen and brilliant editor Kathy Yanni. I went on to thank Tremper, my children, and mostly my wife, Becky.

I doubt many people read the acknowledgments, though it is one of the first sections of a book I read. I couldn't care less who endorses the book. We all know what a necessary part of sales it is. I don't really look at the chapter headings or even the preface, until I read whom the author thanks and how she does so.

Books are written by a person and at times, like this volume, coauthors. Who are they? Why did they write? What is the journey this book, if finished, will take me on? My first glimpse to that end is what I read in the acknowledgments.

Let me tell you up front that the group of names from the

first volume is not the same for the reprint. Instead, I thank my colleagues in The Allender Center of Abuse and Trauma: Cathy Loerzel, Jeanette White, Wendell Moss, Susan Kim, Abby Wong, Trapper Lukaart, Andy Ide, and Rachael Clinton. They are young, passionate, and wise soul laborers who know what it is to sing death and resurrection. They live and breath the freedom and power of the ascension.

If you are a careful, somewhat curious reader you may wonder how a coauthored book is written. We have chosen to divide the chapters and then turn the chapter over to the other to rewrite, to be turned back to be rewritten again and again until we are satisfied each chapter reflects our individual convictions.

The process is tedious, but it leads to a confidence that the opinions expressed reflect our joint authorship. That requires a superb working relationship—a deep trust, and a willingness to dialogue, argue, ponder. This book reflects interactions that have spanned twenty-nine years. There are no words that can express my gratitude to Tremper for faithfully, winsomely loving me through days of tumult and loss, seasons of sin and failure. An ongoing, deepening friendship of nearly fifty years is a treasure that is second only to my wife and family.

My deepest thanks are reserved for those who bear the hardest weight in the process—my family. Anna, you are a stunning mother, wife, and caregiver for your patients. You have no idea how deeply I adore your heart. Amanda, you are a mysterious, kind-hearted thirty-year-old. Your passion for life brings your husband and your family joy. Andrew, you are a brilliant father, husband, and friend. You have become a man I love and respect, and I wish I had been more like you when I was younger.

And finally, love of my life, Rebecca, no one draws my heart to the passion of heaven, no one can break my heart or give me a taste of glory, like you. Your life is a gift exceeded only by the promise of an eternity with you. I am grateful that you struggle faithfully to know God and offer the fruits of your journey to your family.

Dan Allender

When Dan and I started the first edition of this book, we foolishly thought that it would be an easy, manageable project. Little did we know that God had other ideas.

We presumed to write on dark emotions, and God allowed our lives to be the proving ground for our developing convictions. We have felt God plow us up, cut furrows in us, and bring forth fruit that we hope will nourish those who are willing to grow with us. It has been an intense, difficult process.

On October 1, 1993, our good friend Ray Dillard died at age forty-nine. Ray lived a life of service and passion surpassed by few. We both first met Ray as new students at Westminster Theological Seminary in 1974. He was only nine years older than we were, but he had a maturity and wisdom that surpassed his chronological age. As our teacher he had a tremendous influence on both our lives.

He encouraged me to pursue graduate studies in Old Testament and then hired me as his colleague. Ray, Dan, and I made that rare transition from respected teacher/student to intimate friendship. On the occasion of publication of the second edition, we still feel the loss of his presence in our lives over twenty years later.

In the almost two decades since the publication of the first edition, our lives, like the lives of all of our readers, have experienced great joys as well as tremendous struggles.

My three sons were sixteen, fourteen, and ten when this book first appeared. Tremper IV is now thirty-seven and the wonderful father of two beautiful girls, Gabrielle (ten) and Mia (six). In the midst of a full work schedule, as well as raising his girls, he has studied hard and we will be celebrating his MBA (with honors) in about a month. Our now thirty-four-year-old Timothy married Kari this year, and we are so happy to have this wonderful woman in our family. Tim practices antitrust law in Washington, DC, and Kari helps manage a local non-profit. Andrew, our youngest, just turned thirty-one and is married to the talented Tiffany. They too live in DC, where Andrew is in private banking and Tiffany is a clinical psychologist. We are so proud of all of our children, their wives, and our granddaughters.

My friendship with Dan over the years (has it really been fifty years since we first became best friends?) has been a rare privilege, a true token of God's grace. I owe much to Dan, not least that he made me, shy around girls as a freshman in college, to act on my desires and ask a certain Alice Scheetz (now Longman for the past forty-two years) out on a date. It was then about thirty years ago when Dan inspired me to be an academic who brought whatever I had to the service of the church and individual lives. I could have spent the rest of my life in the ivory tower studying the text and writing esoteric articles and books (I've done a few of those too), but he encouraged me to consider the importance of bringing the text to real lives, including my own.

Like Dan, I too want to thank Kathy Yanni, our original editor. Not only can she carefully craft a manuscript, but she can also talk and play baseball—an incredible combination. We also appreciate Don Pape, who offered to bring out this second edition and who brought the process to a conclusion. And words cannot express our gratitude to Joni Eareckson Tada for her moving preface to the second edition.

Finally, and most importantly, my wife, Alice, is the greatest gift God has given me. She is beautiful in appearance and in personality. She believes in me, and she has encouraged my labor—far more, she lives with a depth of love that I yearn to mimic. The best decision I ever made was marrying her when we were a mere twenty—all the more years to enjoy together.

Tremper Longman III

ABOUT THE AUTHORS

DR. DAN B. ALLENDER travels and speaks extensively to present his unique perspective on sexual abuse recovery, love and forgiveness, worship, and related topics. He is author of the bestselling *Wounded Heart* and has coauthored several books with Dr. Tremper Longman: *Intimate Allies*, *Bold Love*, *Bold Purpose*, and *God Loves Sex*. In 2010, The Allender Center was launched as a nonprofit organization within The Seattle School of Theology & Psychology, where Dan is dedicated to the training of counseling professionals working in the areas of trauma and abuse. He is the father of three adult children and lives on Bainbridge Island with his wife, Becky. Dan and Becky have three grandchildren.

DR. TREMPER LONGMAN III (BA Ohio Wesleyan University; MDiv Westminster Theological Seminary; MPhil and PhD Yale University) is the Robert H. Gundry Professor of Biblical Studies at Westmont College. He has written over twenty-five books, including commentaries on Job, Psalms, Proverbs, Ecclesiastes, Song of Songs, Jeremiah, Lamentations, Daniel, and Nahum. In addition, as a Hebrew scholar, he is one of the main translators of the New Living Translation of the Bible and has served as a consultant on other popular translations of the Bible, including *The Message*, the New Century Version, the Holman Christian Standard Bible, and the Common English Bible. Tremper is married to Alice and has three sons (Tremper, Timothy, and Andrew) and two granddaughters (Gabrielle and Mia).

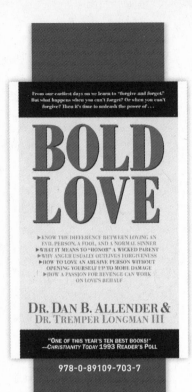